Johnny Antonelli
*A Baseball
Memoir*

JOHNNY ANTONELLI

A Baseball Memoir

by
Johnny Antonelli
and
Scott Pitoniak

 RIT PRESS ✪ ROCHESTER, NEW YORK

This book is made possible, in part, by support from the
Bower Family Publication Fund at RIT.

RIT Press
90 Lomb Memorial Drive
Rochester, New York 14623-5604
http://carypress.rit.edu

Book and cover design by Marnie Soom
Cover photo courtesy of Johnny Antonelli
Printed in the U.S.A. by Thomson-Shore

ISBN 978-1-933360-61-4

Library of Congress Cataloging-in-Publication Data

Antonelli, Johnny.
  Johnny Antonelli : a baseball memoir / Johnny Antonelli and Scott
Pitoniak.
     p. cm.
  Includes index.
  ISBN 978-1-933360-61-4 (alk. paper)
  1. Antonelli, Johnny. 2. Baseball players—United States—Biography.
  3. Pitchers (Baseball)—United States—Biography. I. Pitoniak, Scott.
  II. Title.
  GV865.A7A3 2012
  796.357092—dc23
  [B]
                              2012006905

To my father's faith in me, my family, my friends and my fans.
Johnny Antonelli

To my favorite home team — Beth, Amy, Chris & Sassy
Scott Pitoniak

CONTENTS

INTRODUCTION

I DON'T REMEMBER WHEN I FIRST MET JOHNNY ANTONELLI. But it had to be the early 1990s and it probably was over a heaping plate of rigatoni and meatballs at a popular Italian restaurant in a Rochester, New York, neighborhood that had seen better days. John Ricco, a fan of my newspaper columns but a total stranger at the time, called me out of the blue one day and said that he and a handful of sports legends, including Antonelli, gathered every so often for lunch at a place called Antonetta's on Jay Street and asked me if I would like to join them.

In less time than it took one of those trademark Antonelli fastballs from the 1950s to zip from the long fingers of his left hand into the catcher's mitt, I answered "yes," and thus began a few-times-a-year tradition I fondly refer to as "lunches with legends." And what legends they truly were. Besides Antonelli, a five-time All-Star pitcher for the New York and San Francisco Giants, these informal get-togethers included the likes of world boxing champion Carmen Basilio, U.S. Amateur Open golf champ Sam Urzetta and Naismith Basketball Hall of Famer Al Cervi.

I have always been a history buff and often gravitate to athletes of earlier eras because I find their stories more compelling, richer in detail and more humorous than the ones I hear from current-day athletes. I clearly was in my glory as I listened to these aging sports warriors spin tall tales and joke with one another. Although I was the young whippersnapper of the group and brought little to the table as far as athletic achievements were concerned, they made me feel right at home. I immediately hit it off with Antonelli because baseball had always been my favorite sport. He liked to razz Ricco and me about our longtime allegiances to the New York Yankees. We jokingly fired back that if Johnny had signed with the Bronx Bombers instead of the Boston Braves in the summer of 1948, he would have been wearing ten World Series rings, and, he—*not* Whitey Ford—might have become known as the Yankees' "Chairman of the Board."

Each lunch, Johnny would regale us with marvelous anecdotes about what it was like to play during that golden era of baseball when New York City, boasting the Yankees, Dodgers and Giants, truly was the sport's epicenter. He weaved stories about iconic people (Willie Mays, Jackie Robinson, Leo Durocher, Ted Williams, Mickey Mantle and Stan Musial) and places (the Polo Grounds, Ebbets Field, Yankee Stadium). We would laugh lustily as Johnny joked self-deprecatingly about how light-hitting Cleveland Indians' leadoff hitter Al Smith smashed Antonelli's very first World Series pitch over the roof for a home run. "Now, there's a record that can never be broken," Johnny said, grinning impishly. "It can only be tied." He told us how he and fellow nineteen-year-old teammate, Del Crandall, became the youngest battery (pitcher and catcher) in baseball history to win a game. And he pointed with pride to the seventeen career home runs he hit in the big leagues, claiming that the *Baseball Encyclopedia's* notation that he only hit fifteen had to be in error. "I know I'm right," he said, smiling, "because pitchers can't hit, so we never forget the times we smack the long ball."

In 2004, on the fiftieth anniversary of Antonelli's signature season when he played a major role in helping the Giants win not only the pennant, but the World Series, I wrote a long column for the *Democrat and Chronicle* sports section about his vastly underrated baseball career. At that time, I was working on a number of book projects, but the seed had been planted for a book about Antonelli because the historian in me wanted to make sure his achievements and anecdotes would be preserved for posterity.

The problem was that I didn't know if Johnny would necessarily want to do a book because he is such a humble guy. And it is one thing to tell tales among friends and quite another to spin yarns for all the world to read. Fortunately, he graciously accepted.

One of only seventeen major league players never to have spent a single day in the minors, Johnny was a highly coveted phenom who signed a "bonus baby" contract with the Boston Braves for $52,000 a few days after graduating from Rochester's Jefferson High School in 1948. It wasn't until six years later—when he was traded to the New York Giants after a couple of inauspicious seasons with the Braves and a two-year stint in the Army—that the stylish left-hander began realizing the potential the scouts had seen in him. In a seven-year stretch— from 1953-59—Antonelli was among baseball's best hurlers, compiling a 114-89 record, twenty-three shutouts and nine saves. He was named to the National League All-Star squad five times, won twenty games twice and paced the senior circuit in shutouts two times. He also became the first pitcher in baseball history to record a win and a save in both World Series and All-Star Game competition. (The only other pitcher to match that feat is Hall of Fame reliever Bruce Sutter.)

Antonelli's signature season was 1954, when he went 21-7 with six shutouts and a league-leading 2.30 earned run average, and picked up a win and a save in the Giants four-game World Series sweep against the heavily favored Cleveland Indians. There was no Cy Young Award in those days, but if there had been, he would have won it in a landslide. *The Sporting News,* which was recognized as the Bible of Baseball, named him Major League Pitcher of the Year.

Despite receiving a lucrative contract offer from the upstart New York Mets in 1962, Antonelli retired from the game just before his thirty-second birthday. A devoted husband and family man, he had grown tired of the travel (by this time the Giants had moved to San Francisco) and he wanted to plunge fulltime into his tire business, prompting new Mets manager Casey Stengel to joke to reporters: "I guess Johnny Antonelli is doing all right selling those black doughnuts in Rochester."

Antonelli was indeed doing all right as an entrepreneur. Unlike many of his baseball peers who believed they were immortal and would play forever, Johnny began plotting his second career while still playing ball. He invested his World Series winnings from 1954 in his first Firestone store and worked hard at building the business, particularly on the commercial side, landing accounts with the likes of film giant Eastman Kodak Company and the local postal service. At its peak, Antonelli's tire empire featured twenty-eight stores and employed nearly three hundred fulltime workers.

He sold the multimillion dollar business twenty years ago, but remains quite active in retirement.

Although a balky back prevents the distinguished-looking eighty-two-year-old from playing golf any more (he was good enough to win some local tournaments and shoot a seventy-one at the nation's top-rated course, Oak Hill Country Club), Johnny keeps busy traveling with his wife, Gail, to and from their homes in suburban Rochester and Santa Fe, New Mexico. He also enjoys kibitzing with friends, watching his grandchildren and great-grandchildren pursue their various activities, and viewing baseball games on television.

Despite being annoyed with the plodding pace of today's contests, fueled by innumerable pitching changes, Johnny still loves the game.

"I owe everything I have to baseball," he has told me on numerous occasions. "It has enabled me to live a wonderful life."

In the following pages, we look back on that wonderful life. Here's hoping this memoir reads as if you are sitting at a table with Johnny at Antonetta's, enjoying a bountiful plate of pasta and the delicious tales of a fruitful journey.

Enjoy!
Scott Pitoniak

CHAPTER 1
FULFILLING A DREAM

I LIKE TO JOKE THAT IF IT WEREN'T FOR MY DAD I WOULD HAVE spent my life brown bagging it at Kodak. Not that there would have been anything wrong with working for the company that made photography famous worldwide and used to be Rochester, New York's, largest employer. It's just that without my dad's lobbying efforts I never would have gotten the opportunity to impress the scouts and realize my boyhood dream of becoming a big-league baseball player.

August Antonelli—everybody called him "Gus"—was born in Casalbordino, a small village in the province of Abruzzi, on the Adriatic side of Italy, about a hundred miles east of Rome. He came to the United States when he was about thirteen so he could be reunited with my grandfather who had arrived here a few years earlier and had landed a job as a railroad foreman in Buffalo.

It couldn't have been easy for Dad, leaving Italy as a young teenager and traveling halfway around the world on an ocean liner with thousands of strangers. A lot of people became sick and died before ever seeing the Statue of Liberty in New York's harbor. Fortunately, my dad made it to Ellis Island with his health intact, and after going through processing, he figured out which train would take him to Buffalo. Even at that young age, Pops was a self-assured, independent-minded person. Knowing how to speak and read English obviously made his journey a little easier.

Dad's understanding of the language also proved to be a great asset to my grandfather, who was not at all fluent in English. Grandpa

1

Antonelli immediately put Dad to work, handling time cards and other paper work as well as serving as an interpreter.

One day, when he was in his early twenties, Dad was walking down a street in Buffalo, looking for a cup of coffee, when, through the window of an ice cream parlor, he spotted a young lady scooping ice cream from a vat. My dad liked what he saw so much that he walked past the window several times before getting up the courage to go into the parlor and introduce himself. Her parents also were from Italy, so they hit it off right away. About a year later, Josephine Messore and Gus Antonelli were married in Buffalo.

Mom apparently was a pretty good cook because in that first year of marriage, Dad put on a hundred pounds. I'm not making that up. He really did gain that much weight, and, sadly, was never able to take it off, which led to health problems later in life.

For about five years, they lived in Buffalo, where my older brother, Anthony, and my older sister, Lucy, were born. Dad did extremely well with the railroad company and wound up receiving several promotions, including one that required us to move to Rochester, where I was born on April 12, 1930.

My dad may have opened the door to my baseball career, but my mom deserves a lot of credit, too. In reality, you could argue that my athletic genes come from her side of the family. My Uncle Chuck was a good enough catcher to land a tryout with the Syracuse Chiefs of the International League, and my Uncle Nick was a pretty fair semi-pro shortstop. My Aunt Anna was an excellent athlete who attended Indiana University when Cincinnati Reds slugger Ted Kluszewski was a star football and baseball player there. She wound up earning a degree in physical education and later became the athletic director of Kensington High School in Buffalo. I believe she was one of the first women in the entire state to run a high school athletic department. And my Uncle Anthony was plenty talented, too, but his athletic career was cut short by World War II, when he wound up being the bombardier on a plane piloted by the legendary actor Clark Gable.

My mother was a gifted athlete, too. At 5-foot-8, she was as tall as my dad, but obviously much, much thinner and more nimble. Josephine Antonelli excelled at badminton, and became so proficient at it that she eventually teamed with F. Ritter Shumway to win several doubles championships in the Rochester area. When I was very young, I would tag along with her and watch her teach badminton classes at the local schools. Even into her eighties she'd be out there shooting baskets with her grandchildren. This is not to say that Dad didn't have any athletic skills. He was as strong as an ox with big, broad shoulders and a blacksmith's forearms. He became a decent bowler, with a league average in the 180s. But looking back, I'd definitely have to give my mom's family a decided edge when it came to athletic prowess. They were all good athletes.

We initially lived on Adams Street in the Corn Hill section of Rochester, but moved to Ambrose Street between Lake and Plymouth avenues when I was two. We stayed on Ambrose—we lived in two different houses there—until 1943 when we moved to Ravine Avenue off of Dewey Avenue.

The neighborhoods where I grew up were primarily comprised of Italian, Irish and German immigrant families. And the thing I remember most is how our house became a gathering spot. The doors were always open, and people were always stopping by to visit. I think part of it had to do with the generosity of my parents. Mom and Dad were always making things and giving them away to neighbors, relatives and co-workers. Dad would buy everything—apples, pears, peaches, tomatoes—by the bushel. And my mom would put them into cans. I swear she would can at least three hundred cans of tomatoes a year.

My dad also made his own wine. And the funny thing about that is that he didn't drink alcohol. (I guess that helps explain why I became a teetotaler , too.) Dad would make two barrels of red wine and one of white wine. After they fermented, he would put them in five-gallon jugs and cork and wax them so the air wouldn't get in. Then, he would call his friends, co-workers and people he did business with and tell them he had a gallon of wine for them. And he wouldn't stop there. He'd tell them that he also had a brick of cheese or a basket of peaches or pears for them. He took great pride in his wine and his food baskets. And he gave all of them away. He wasn't looking to make a buck. It was just the way my parents were. Very giving people.

We didn't have computers or video games back then—heck, we

didn't get a television until I was a teenager—but we never felt like we were lacking for things to do when I was growing up. Sports were a big deal in our neighborhood and we always seemed to be outdoors playing something, regardless of the weather. And there was no adult supervision needed. We'd police ourselves, and everything worked out just fine that way.

There was a coalfield just down the hill from our house on Ambrose Street, and we'd play baseball there because it was closer and more convenient than going several blocks away to Tacoma Park or School No. 30. The grounds were owned by the gas and electric company. It's where they stored the coal they used for making power. They would scrape it and grade it whenever they were loading coal into the trucks, so it usually was a pretty level surface to play on, but it wasn't a place you'd want to slide or dive for balls. My friends and I were forced to pick many a cinder from scrapes and cuts we incurred, but we didn't care. It was our home diamond, so to speak, and the men who operated the heavy equipment and trucks were fine with us using the grounds, so it worked out well.

Our equipment wasn't exactly what you would call state of the art. We'd use hand-me-down gloves and when the balls started to unravel, we'd wrap black electrician's tape around them and keep using them. And if we cracked a bat, we'd simply get a nail or a screw and hammer it back together. No big deal. You just made do with what you had.

My first baseball glove actually was one that I found at an empty ball field near Lyell Avenue. You would have thought I had discovered a crisp, new fifty-dollar bill instead of a beaten-up piece of leather; that's how happy I was with my discovery. It was a right-handed glove and I threw left-handed, but I didn't care. I just wore it on my right hand. It got the job done. Eventually, my dad got me a new glove—I think it cost three dollars—and it was made for left-handed throwers. It's still one of the best gifts I've ever received.

I joke that I'm a lefthander who thinks right-handed because we all know how strange southpaws can be. The funny thing is that I'm somewhat ambidextrous. I threw, batted and played golf left-handed, but I ate, wrote and played badminton and tennis right-handed. Go figure.

We didn't have Little League Baseball back then. In fact, I didn't really play organized hardball until I was in junior high. Eastman Kodak Company sponsored the Kodak Park Athletic Association, a/k/a KPAA. It was run by Harold "Shifty" Gears, who had been one of the greatest fast pitch softball pitchers of all time and who had helped Kodak win two world championships. It was a wonderful program, and when we weren't playing there, you'd find us playing ball, sunrise to sunset, at the coalfield or the playgrounds.

To be honest with you, I don't know how my dad became interested in baseball. But I think he was like a lot of immigrants at the time. Baseball truly was our national pastime back then and if you wanted to assimilate into the American society, there was no faster way to do that than by learning about and following baseball. Plus, I think my dad looked at the box scores in the newspaper and was intrigued to find Italian names like Lazzeri, Crosetti, DiMaggio and Berra. For as long as I can remember, he loved the game and he certainly passed along that love to me.

Like a lot of people in Rochester back in the 1930s and 1940s, I was a huge St. Louis Cardinals fan. They were the parent club of the Red Wings and many of the guys who had played Triple-A baseball in Rochester—players like Stan Musial, Marty Marion and Whitey Kurowski—eventually wound up playing for St. Louis in the big leagues. Of all the players, my favorite was probably a guy named Harry Davis because he was a first baseman and that was my position, too, early on.

I don't remember the first game I attended at old Red Wing Stadium on Norton Street, but I had to be just a kid. I do have vivid memories of games against Newark, the Yankees top minor league affiliate. They were loaded with great players like Yogi Berra and King Kong Keller. Heck, they were so good they could beat any team in the big leagues, including the Yankees. The crowds were so big for some of those Newark games at Red Wing Stadium that they would rope off the outfield and let people sit out there, just to be able to squeeze a few thousand more people into the park. If a player hit it into that area it would be a ground-rule double.

One of the best parts about going to games is that my dad would always buy me a bag of peanuts. It's funny, but to this day, whenever

I go to a game, I have to buy a bag of peanuts and crack open the shells. Call it an Antonelli tradition.

I remember one time Pops took me to Red Wing Stadium to watch the Kansas City Monarchs of the old Negro Leagues play an exhibition against Rochester. One of the Monarchs' players was Buck O'Neil, who would later gain fame for the wonderful stories he told throughout Ken Burns' critically acclaimed PBS series about baseball. This, of course, was several years before the major leagues were integrated. And I remember not understanding why these guys weren't allowed to play in the big leagues with the white ballplayers because they seemed awfully talented to me.

Like I said, I didn't play organized baseball until I was a freshman at Jefferson High School. One day during infield practice, I was wheeling around making the throws from first base to home when the varsity coach, Charlie O'Brien, noticed there was a lot of movement on the balls I threw. He asked me if ever pitched, and I told him, "No. I'm a first baseman because I like playing every day." He said, "Well, I notice your throws have a nice tail on them, so I'm going to have Pat Arioli work with you a little bit as a pitcher." I grudgingly gave it a try, but deep down in my heart, I wanted to stay at first base because I knew that pitchers only played some times, and I wanted to be out there all the time, every game. Looking back, I'm happy Coach noticed I had a "live arm" because as much as I liked hitting and playing first base, I doubt I would have made it as far as I did if I didn't switch to my natural position.

I had great coaches at Jefferson. In fact, I learned more baseball from Coach O'Brien and teammates like Arioli than I did at any other point in my career—and that includes my twelve seasons in the major leagues when I played with and for several guys who would wind up being enshrined in the Baseball Hall of Fame in Cooperstown. Coach O'Brien had been up for a cup of coffee in the big leagues, and he knew the game inside and out. We had the fundamentals down pat. We backed up throws, knew how to bunt and slide, moved runners over and hit the cut-off man. I was very fortunate to play for guys who were so knowledgeable about the game.

Though baseball was my first love and my best sport, I also played football, basketball and volleyball at Jefferson. The highlight of my career on the gridiron came against East High School in the city championship game, which in those days was played in front of several thousand spectators at Red Wing Stadium. We were on our own seventeen-yard-line in the fourth quarter of a scoreless tie when Coach O'Brien sent in a play called "Johnny's Long Pass." In those days, I could throw the ball about sixty yards, and Coach figured it was time to let me air one out. The play called for me to be at halfback and take a direct snap from center, then roll right and hit Cosmo Trotto—a great friend who wound up being the best man in my wedding—about thirty yards down field. Well, they snap me the ball and Cosmo wound up being open right away, so I started calling his name and tossed the ball to him immediately. He went the distance and we won 6-0.

Jefferson was a high school sports powerhouse in those days, but we weren't that great at basketball. I was co-captain of the team my senior year and wound up making the citywide all-star team as an honorable mention. One of my most memorable games was against East High and its 6-foot-11 center, Walter Dukes, who would go on to play at Seton Hall University and in the National Basketball Association for several seasons. He had almost a foot on me and one of our teammates. But we double-teamed Dukes and wound up getting him into foul trouble. At one point, we led by twelve points, but the upset wasn't to be as Dukes came back in and East rallied to beat us.

The basketball season usually was over in February and they would have a volleyball season before the spring sports started up. I played that, too, and we wound up winning a city championship.

High school sports were different back then. Unlike today, where so many athletes, especially the gifted ones, seem to specialize in one sport year-round, we played multiple sports. And I think that was good because it prevented you from overdoing it and burning out. And I believe the skill sets in one sport help you perform well in other sports.

One of my other loves growing up was music. People are surprised when I tell them I also sang in the school choir and played the trumpet. I wasn't great at either, but I enjoyed playing and singing in concerts at Jefferson. I gave up the trumpet when I was about sixteen, but I still have it in my possession. And, later, when I attended

Bowling Green University for a year, I actually majored in music and physical education. I was about a C-plus student, and probably could have done better had I studied more. I loved history and math, but when we got to subjects like trigonometry and geometry I struggled. I had some problems with my eyes that made it difficult for me to read for long periods of time. Still, I probably could have done better had I studied a little harder.

As I mentioned, my initial dream was to become a first baseman, but Coach O'Brien immediately saw something in me that I didn't see in myself and switched me to pitcher. I don't remember all the particulars of the first game I pitched. I do know that it was a junior varsity game against Charlotte and I wound up striking out a dozen batters and yielding two or three hits. That debut definitely was a big boost to my confidence, and made me want to work on becoming the best pitcher I could.

I played a lot of catch after that to strengthen my arm. And as time passed and I put on a few pounds, my fastball really started to explode past hitters. By my junior season, I had become a dominating pitcher. According to newspaper accounts that spring, I struck out 132 batters and yielded just fifteen walks and nineteen hits in fifty-five innings. Because of bad weather, I only pitched thirty-six innings my senior season, but still wound up with seventy-four strikeouts, while yielding only nine hits and three walks. During my three-year varsity career at Jefferson, I threw three no-hitters, five one-hitters, posted a 15-3 won-lost record and struck out 278 batters in just 129 innings.

It's funny, but despite all the success I enjoyed with the Jeffs, it's those three games I lost that I remember most vividly all these years later. One of them came against Madison High School's Andy Spennachio. He was a heck of a shortstop, and when their ace pitcher got sick, Andy came in and shut us down. My other two losses were to West High School's Billy Allen, a 6-foot-4 flame-thrower who wound up signing with the Boston Braves in 1949. He never got out of their minor league system, but did become a heck of an amateur golfer in Rochester. Billy and I locked horns in one of the best high school games ever played in the Flower City. He beat me 1-0 in front of a crowd of 4,023 at Red Wing Stadium, throwing a no-hitter to my one-hitter. He had twelve strikeouts and I had sixteen. It was one of the toughest losses for me to swallow, and that includes all the games I pitched in the big leagues.

Like I said before, my dad was the driving force behind my baseball career. He didn't force me to play—he didn't have to because I loved the game with heart and soul. But he did create opportunities for me that enabled me to make my dream of playing ball for a living come true. When I was just fourteen or fifteen, he arranged for me to participate in a tryout camp the St. Louis Cardinals were staging at Red Wing Stadium. There were about a hundred players in the camp, and although I was the youngest, the Cardinals scouts named me the top player. I think that was the first time I showed up on their radar screen and it got the ball rolling for me.

As a result of my performance in that camp, I was invited to pitch on an amateur all-star team in the Hearst National Championship Game in the Polo Grounds in New York City. I wound up doing extremely well in that game, and afterward, Dutch Ruether, a scout with the Chicago Cubs, told a reporter that I was the best pitching discovery since Bob Feller.

The following summer, Paul Krichell, the famed Yankees scout who signed Lou Gehrig, Whitey Ford and Phil Rizzuto among others, visited Rochester to watch me pitch for the Flower City American Legion Post. I only threw for five innings in that game, but I guess that outing was long enough to impress him. "Invite me to your high school graduation," Krichell said, while shaking my hand after the game.

"Why?" I asked.

"'Cause on that night I want to offer you a contract."

My mom would keep elaborate scrapbooks with newspaper clippings chronicling all these heady events. The stories in the local papers often referred to me as "the curly-thatched, teenaged southpaw" or by the nicknames reporters and friends had bestowed upon me— "Anty," "Aunty Nelly" or "Johnny the Kid." When my dad started making trips to the major league spring training camps, he'd take those scrapbooks with him. He'd show general managers and scouts and players the clippings and tell them they should come up to Rochester and take a look at his boy. One time, he even showed the stories to Feller, the great Cleveland Indians pitcher, and he told Dad, "Geez, that's a better record than I had in high school."

I was a shy kid who didn't like to brag about his accomplishments, so I was a little embarrassed. But I realized my dad was just trying to help me get my foot in the door so I could enjoy a better, more prosperous life than he had.

Railroad construction was hard, backbreaking work, as my brother Anthony and I discovered, when Dad put us on his crew during summers when we were teenagers. Every yard of those iron tracks weighed 110 pounds and they were thirty-three feet long. It would take twelve of us—six on each side—to pick up one of those rails and put it in place. Then, you'd have to drill holes and drive spikes into wooden support planks. On a couple of occasions, I saw my dad grab a sledgehammer and demonstrate how it was supposed to be done. Bam! Bam! Bam! He'd drive that spike through with seeming ease. It was an impressive display of strength and accuracy. Most of the time, though, my dad was the foreman overseeing the laying of tracks. Drive around Rochester today and you're bound to cross over some railroad track that my dad was responsible for. I'm proud of that, and I'm also grateful I was gifted enough to play major league baseball because working on the railroad was not an easy life.

People told me that Dad's sales campaign really started to take off after he persuaded Dan Parker, a respected columnist for the *New York Daily Mirror*, to write about this diamond-in-the-rough, left-handed pitcher in little old Rochester. Parker's column was syndicated in newspapers across the country and it clearly stoked the scouts' interest in me.

After that, Dad was contacted by a coach from the Vermont hotel summer baseball league, which featured some of the top high school and college players in the country. Playing there for the Rutland team the summer before my senior year was great exposure for me and enabled me to test myself against some of the nation's premier amateur players. The Vermont league was like the Cape Cod League is today. When you weren't playing ball, they'd find some menial work for you to do, and your food and lodgings were taken care of by the hotels that sponsored the teams. I wound up being managed by Ebba St.

Claire, who later would be one of my Braves teammates and would be traded with me to the Giants. I didn't get off to a great start—I lost the first game I pitched. But I settled down and I guess I impressed Ebba, who told a reporter near the end of the season, "I'm perfectly satisfied with the kid. He has the makings of a great pitcher." Veteran umpire Red Gendron added that, "in all my years in this loop, I've never seen a youngster with so much stuff." It was a great learning experience for me, on and off the field. It definitely got me prepared not only for pro ball, but for being away from home for long stretches of time, which is a big part of the baseball player's experience.

CHAPTER 2

BECOMING A "BONUS BABY"

FOR THE PAST FOUR DECADES THERE'S BEEN AN AMATEUR player draft in major league baseball in which teams pick in descending order, depending on their record from the previous season. So the team with the worst record chooses first, followed by the team with the second-worst record, and so on. But back in the late 1940s, there wasn't a draft, so you could sign with whomever you wanted. You were a free agent. But you couldn't put your John Hancock on a contract until after you graduated from high school.

As my high school graduation approached in late June 1948, my father came up with a brilliant idea that wound up making me tens of thousands of dollars. To showcase my pitching skills for the scouts, he arranged for me to pitch an exhibition game at Red Wing Stadium against a team of highly skilled semi-pro baseball players. It was a calculated risk, to be sure, because our high school season had ended a few weeks earlier and I hadn't picked up a ball since. So, there was the danger I would be rusty. There also was the chance these seasoned players, many in their late twenties, early thirties, might knock me around the park, in which case I'd no longer be a hot commodity and I would have to sign for peanuts.

But Dad was confident in my ability to seize this opportunity, and so was I.

With just over 7,700 spectators and more than a dozen scouts and general managers in the stands, I took the mound for the Rochester Stars against the Brockport Barons on June 18 in what would turn out to be the most important game of my life. Yeah, I was nervous. Who wouldn't be? I was just eighteen years old and I was putting my life-long dream on the line.

But I settled down the minute I delivered my first pitch and wound up turning in one of my best performances. The ball was coming out of my hand nice and easy and I was blowing it by the hitters with relative ease. I mowed down the first nine guys I faced and figured I was done for the night. But the scouts came up to my father and said, "We want to see more." So I pitched another few innings, and I thought I was done again, but they told my dad, "We pay guys to pitch nine innings in the big leagues, so we want to see if your boy has the endurance to go the distance." Back out I went, and when it was over, I had struck out seventeen batters en route to a no-hitter. I also contributed two hits as we won, 11-0. My dad was ecstatic, the scouts obviously were impressed and I was relieved.

Our high stakes gamble had paid off. We discovered just how much so the following day.

Each of the club representatives was given a time to meet with my dad at the kitchen table of our modest, two-story house on 397 Ravine Avenue. It really was kind of surreal watching the sweepstakes unfold. It also was kind of surreal knowing that you were the item being auctioned to the highest bidder. There was my mom, feeding each visitor delicious homemade pasta, bread and soup, and there was my dad listening to each man's sales pitch. This was an era long before agents, but my dad was just like one. He may not have gone to college, but he was a very bright guy. He had street smarts and he knew how to read people really well. He was a very skilled negotiator. The men from the big cities quickly discovered they weren't dealing with some country bumpkin.

One by one, they showed up for their individual audiences with my dad. I remember the Yankees' rep, Johnny Haddock, being there, and I know Dad was hoping he would make the best offer because the Bronx Bombers were his favorite team. I would have loved to play with Joe DiMaggio and Yogi Berra and Phil Rizzuto. Plus, Yankee Stadium was close enough to Rochester that my family and friends would be able to hop in their cars or on the train and see me play. But the Yankees only offered about $30,000.

"That's lower than what we've been promised by other teams," Dad told Haddock.

"But Mr. Antonelli," he responded, "we are the New York Yankees and what you have to understand is that we go to the World Series almost every year, so your son will be receiving a nice bonus each time we do."

To his credit, Dad stuck to his guns. He was seeking the best offer, and he felt the Yankees were low-balling us.

One of my big thrills of the day was meeting Carl Hubbell, the Hall of Fame pitcher who struck out legends Babe Ruth, Lou Gehrig, Jimmie Foxx, Al Simmons and Joe Cronin in succession during the 1934 All-Star game—still regarded as one of the greatest feats in baseball history. King Carl, as he was known during his playing days, had told reporters that I had the best all-around stuff he had ever seen. I was floored when that comment was relayed to me. After exchanging pleasantries with us, Hubbell, the farm director of the New York Giants at the time, entered a bid of $41,000 for my services, topping the Yankees offer, but not going quite high enough in my dad's estimation.

Interestingly, we also received an offer of about $20,000 from the Rochester Red Wings. Their general manager, Joe Ziegler, obviously would have loved to have signed me, figuring I'd be a big drawing card in my hometown and that the Wings would more than make up for the money they paid me from the big crowds they thought I would draw. It was a nice gesture and good publicity for the Wings, but their front office realized they weren't going to be able to compete with the money the big league teams would be putting up.

The Boston Red Sox were represented by their top scout, Specs Toporcer, who had been an outstanding player for the Red Wings in his day. He showed us a contract for about $50,000 and told my dad to call him if anybody matched the offer. His exact words were: "Gus, I'm not leaving town without your son's signature on a contract. We really want him to play for the Boston Red Sox, and I'd like the chance to bid again if anyone surpasses this."

As it turned out I did wind up signing with Boston—but not the Red Sox. In those days, Beantown had two big-league clubs: the Red

Sox in the American League and the Braves in the National League. Jeff Jones, the Braves' top scout, had been in the stands for my exhibition game, and he was so impressed with my stuff that he immediately got on the phone with the team's president and co-owner, Lou Perini, and told him, "This is the best pitching prospect I've ever seen. We absolutely have to sign this kid." Perini really respected Jones' opinion—so much so that he hopped aboard his personal plane, a twin-engine Beechcraft, and flew to Rochester to close the deal. I think the fact Lou spoke Italian to my parents and had made his money in the construction business appealed to my dad. It also didn't hurt that the Braves were managed by Billy Southworth, whom my dad had admired for the work he'd done leading the Red Wings to four straight pennants and two minor league World Series titles in the late 1920s and early 1930s. Dad liked Southworth's managing style, and the success he had enjoyed, and felt comfortable that the man with strong ties to the Flower City would take good care of a Rochester boy.

Perini wound up offering us a contract for $52,000. Some reported that it was the biggest bonus ever given to a rookie. But that distinction actually belonged to Curt Simmons, whom the Philadelphia Phillies had signed for $65,000 a few years earlier. My dad accepted the Braves' tender without even getting back to Toporcer, who almost certainly would have made an even bigger offer. I don't know why Dad didn't get back to him, but I know Specs was none too pleased about losing out on me. A few years later, he was in Rochester for some function and he told reporters that I would never realize my baseball potential because I refused to sign for lesser money and spend time in the minor leagues. I felt badly that he felt that way, but I was happy that I wound up proving him wrong.

June 29, 1948, was quite a day for me, my family and our neighbors on Ravine Avenue—a day I'll never forget. Reporters and photographers from both Rochester newspapers—the morning *Democrat and Chronicle* and the afternoon *Times-Union*—were there to capture my signing for posterity. As I scrawled my signature on the contract a little bit past eight o'clock that night, camera flashbulbs exploded. My proud parents and Mr. Perini stood behind me. I don't know who was happier: my dad or me.

"The Boston Braves are delighted to obtain Johnny because he has had such a brilliant career as a schoolboy," Perini told reporters in the impromptu press conference that followed. "If he has what it takes to click in the majors—and my scouts have assured me he has—I know (manager) Billy Southworth will bring him through."

Jones, the Braves chief scout who had coached Newton (Massachusetts) High School to several state baseball championships, then told the press how enthused he became after watching me pitch in that exhibition game at Red Wings Stadium. "In all my career," he said, "I have never seen a young pitcher with such poise as Antonelli possesses." Asked about my big bonus contract, Jones said: "He's worth every cent of it."

Although I appreciated their heartfelt praise, I remember squirming a lot because I was still basically a shy teenager and wasn't comfortable being the center of attention. As a result, I wasn't much of an interview that night. When asked a simple question about how I felt, I nervously told reporters, "Gosh, I hope they keep me."

Times-Union sports editor Matt Jackson captured the mood nicely in the next day's paper when he wrote:

> When it became official "Johnny has signed," it spread around the neighborhood like wildfire. The good neighbors who had been marching up and down, past the Antonelli residence in an effort to sneak a peek, descended en masse to congratulate Johnny. It looked like a celebration for the campus hero.
>
> The joint was buzzing. Everybody had something to say about it. Johnny and his good fortune was community property.
>
> Everybody was sitting on their porches. The neighborhood accordion player squeezed out a trio of song specialties, "Now Is the Hour," "For He's a Jolly Good Fellow" and "Auld Lang Syne," in that order, as Johnny came down the steps for his Boston trip, carrying the traveling bag Owner Lou Perini of the Braves gave him for a graduation present.

The ink had barely dried on the contract when Mr. Perini, my dad, my older brother, Anthony, and I were being whisked to the airport to fly to Boston on the Braves owner's personal plane. I had never flown before, and I can remember the pilot letting me come into the cockpit before we landed at Logan Airport. That was a huge, huge thrill. I couldn't wait to fly again. Ironically, many years and several harrowing flights later, I would grow weary of traveling, and that would be one of the reasons I would give up baseball at the relatively young age of thirty-two.

Like I said, there wasn't a draft in those days, so teams could sign anyone they wanted and as many guys as they wanted. But in order to prevent the wealthiest teams, like the Yankees and the Brooklyn Dodgers, from stockpiling talent, major league baseball instituted a "bonus baby" rule. I don't remember what the cut-off point was, but if you signed a player out of high school for, let's say, $5,000, you had to keep him on your major league roster for a year or two. That would deter teams from signing players to huge bonuses because they wouldn't want to use a roster spot on an untried rookie, particularly if they were a pennant contender.

So by signing me to a "bonus baby" contract, it meant the Braves were going to have to put me on their roster immediately and regardless how I did they wouldn't be able to send me down to the minor leagues for at least two years. If they did try to demote me, they'd have to expose me to waivers, meaning any of the other fifteen clubs in the majors at the time would have an opportunity to claim me for their team.

We arrived in Boston after eleven that night and Perini arranged an informal party where I was introduced to writers from Boston and New York. (The Big Apple reporters were in town because the New York Giants were playing the Braves.) I was extremely nervous. Perini tried to make things easier for me, telling a couple of reporters that I was basically a shy kid. "He's so modest," Perini said. "I think you'll have a hard time getting anything out of him." As it turned out, he was right. I was reluctant to talk about myself, but the writers got plenty of good stuff from Dad. They were especially intrigued about the stories of my father going to spring training to drum up interest in me. "They (major league players, scouts and managers) thought I was crazy—just another father with more pride than common sense," Dad told the reporters that night. "Most of them didn't listen to me at first. Johnny was just a kid then—a sophomore in high school. I couldn't convince anyone at the time that he had it, but they all came flocking around later."

It was well after midnight when we finally got to the hotel and although I was exhausted, I don't remember sleeping much that night because I was so excited. The next day—June 30, 1948—I arrived at Braves Field on the campus of Boston University where Boston played its home games and pulled on a big league uniform for the first time. As I ran my fingers across the white satin jersey that the Braves donned for home night games and looked at the big No. 34 on the back, I tried to digest all that had happened to me in such a short span of time. Here I was, just a few days removed from my high school commencement getting dressed in a big league clubhouse. It still felt like a dream. I was introduced to bullpen catcher Bob Keely, who would be my roommate and mentor. Bob was a good guy who did what he could to make my life easier that season. He took me around and introduced me to the players and manager Billy Southworth. They all seemed nice enough. When I walked onto the field, newspaper photographers immediately asked me to pose for shots with everybody and his brother. I was as nervous as could be, and my nerves didn't really start to settle until the posing was done and I was able to play catch.

In that day's editions, the Boston newspapers called me the second coming of Walter Johnson and played up my signing, especially the fact I was a "bonus baby," erroneously reporting that I had signed for $75,000. I really avoided talking about my contract to reporters or my teammates because I was told it was more money than anybody on the Braves roster was making and I didn't want the established veterans to be resentful of me. And most of them weren't, at least not to my face.

As I would come to learn, being a "bonus baby" was both a blessing and a curse. Obviously, it enabled me to make more money than I ever thought existed before I threw my first pitch in the big leagues. And it also allowed me to be on a major league roster right away. But it also created a lot of resentment because the average player in those days only made around $6,000-$7,000, with the stars in the $20,000-$25,000 range. The super-duper stars—Joe DiMaggio, Ted Williams and Stan Musial—made about $100,000 and they deserved every penny of it because of their abilities to hit the cover off the ball and put fannies in the seats. But they literally were in a league of their own, both skill-wise and salary-wise.

Unlike today, when even mediocre players can make several million a year, we had to make our dollars stretch as far as they could. We'd get six bucks a day in meal money, and many guys would eat at White Tower, where you could get little hamburgers for a dime apiece. You'd spend a dollar on several of those little burgers and a soda and send the other five dollars home to your family. You learned how to be frugal and pinch pennies.

What made my situation more complicated was that I was joining a talented, veteran team in the thick of a pennant race. They already had a pitching rotation stocked with stars such as Warren Spahn, Johnny Sain, Tommy Holmes and Bob Elliott. They had guys who had proved themselves at this level. I hadn't proven a thing. Sain, who was on his way to twenty-four wins that season, was especially upset about my contract. So much so, that a few days after I signed, he stormed into Perini's office and said: "Antonelli may be worth every cent you gave him. But the games he's going to win for the team are in the future. I'm winning them right now. And they may mean a pennant this year. If he's worth that kind of money for tomorrow, I guess I'm worth a lot more today." Perini agreed and I'm told Sain wound up receiving a $9,000 raise to $30,000. Decades later, at a reunion of old Boston Braves players, Sain sought me out and told me that he didn't begrudge me getting the money I did. I told him not to worry about it, that I hadn't taken it personally and was happy that he and some of the other guys were able to use my contract as leverage to get more money.

For some reason, which I still don't understand, Warren Spahn resented me from the start and never stopped. I always showed him the utmost respect and have said on many occasions that he was the greatest southpaw in baseball history. But that didn't seem to matter to Warren. He always treated me with disdain, even when I ran into him years after both of us had stopped playing. He was from Buffalo and my uncles actually were classmates of his at South Park High School. I don't know if he was jealous of my bonus or felt threatened when Perini signed me, but he acted as if I had stolen money from him or had done harm to one of his loved ones. I later learned that Spahn orchestrated my trade from the Braves before the 1954 season. I had rejoined the team in 1953 after a two-year military stint in the army and actually had a solid year going 12-12, a record that could have been much better had I not suffered a bout of pneumonia in the middle of the summer. It appeared that I was finally on my way, but Spahn, who carried a lot of weight because he had become a perennial All-Star, told Perini that the Braves didn't need Antonelli and the owner agreed. It would be a decision that Perini said he wound up regretting and one for which I will always be grateful. But more on that later.

The bonus had made me a marked man, and I wanted so badly to start pitching and earn my keep. But our manager, Billy Southworth, decided to go slowly with me. Part of me understood why. He was in the thick of a pennant race, and he was going to rely on his veteran pitchers. And I would have, too, if I were the manager. But I still think I would have used me more than just four innings—which is all I pitched that season.

It later was reported in a *Sport* magazine article that my signing had caught Southworth off guard. He mistakenly thought I had been signed to a minor league contract. On the ride from the ballpark to the hotel for my first press conference in Boston, Southworth reportedly told a writer: "I suppose they'll put him out with one of our farm clubs for a year. The kid's pea green and he couldn't do anything here but take up space somebody else could use on the roster." The article went on to say that a half hour later, a chagrined Southworth had to change his story when he learned that Perini had signed me to a Braves contract. "I'll just have to find room for him somewhere," was Southworth's response. Not exactly a vote of confidence if you ask me.

But, as I said, I was hankering to get out there and prove them wrong. The last thing in the world I wanted to be was excess baggage, but that's what I became.

I made my major league pitching debut on the Fourth of July 1948 in front of a crowd of 21,861 at Shibe Park in Philadelphia. Southworth put me in to do some mop-up work in the eighth inning of a 7-2 loss to the Phillies in the first game of a doubleheader. I was nervous for sure and wound up yielding a run on two scratch hits and a walk. I didn't pitch again until nine days later in an exhibition game. Each year, the Braves would play a game in Milwaukee against their Triple-A affiliate and Southworth figured this would be a good test for me against one of the best hitting teams in the American Association. I was equal to the task, tossing a three-hit shutout that drew rave reviews from my teammates and the press. I figured I had aced my audition and would start seeing more assignments, but it was not to be.

For the remainder of the season, my work came throwing batting practice for roughly thirty minutes a day, five times a week. Then, when the game started, I would gather splinters on the bench. I wound up pitching only four innings in four games that season, finishing with a 0-0 won-lost record and a 2.25 earned run average. Again, I understood why Southworth might be reluctant to start a young whippersnapper like me when his team was in the midst of a pennant race. If he threw me out there and I lost a crucial game, the press and the fans would be all over him. I just think he could have used me a lot more than he did in mop-up situations so I could have gained some experience.

I was thrilled, though, that we wound up winning the National League pennant, and looked forward to going to the World Series in my first year. But Southworth left me off the Series roster, and that really hurt because I figured all the batting practice work I had done to prepare our hitters for games had contributed in a small way to our success. What hurt even more is that after losing the Series to the Cleveland Indians, my teammates didn't vote me a share of the bonus money given to each player. I truly believe the jealous and threatened Spahn was behind that snub. A few weeks after the season, Major League Baseball Commissioner A.B. "Happy" Chandler righted the wrong and I was awarded a one-eighth share, amounting to $571.34, which was about $250 more than the batboys were awarded. I did receive a World Series ring, like the rest of my teammates, and I eventually gave it to my dad to thank him for all he had done for me. Despite the shenanigans of Spahn and a few others, I looked back on the season with great pride. Heck, I was just eighteen years old and a big league ballplayer, and I looked forward to carrying a much bigger load during my second season.

That October, I fulfilled my parents' wish that I attend college when I enrolled at Bowling Green University where my older brother, Anthony, was a starting fullback and linebacker on an undefeated football team that featured future NFL star Bob Schnelker. Today, Bowling Green has an enrollment of about twenty thousand students, but back then it was a small school, with about one-tenth that total. Combining two of my loves, I signed up for a dual major of physical education and music. Because I was a professional athlete, I wasn't eligible to play any sports in college, but I did spend a lot of time practicing with the basketball team, which was ranked among the nation's best and actually made it all the way to the NCAA finals where it lost to the Adolph Rupp-coached Kentucky team that was later implicated in a point-shaving scandal. I roomed with a couple of the basketball players in a Quonset hut on campus. It's funny, but I don't remember those guys ever going to classes. Around ten o'clock each night, they'd say, 'Hey, let's go shoot some hoops," and we'd head for the gym, where we'd play two-on-two games until one in the morning. Campus security would show up each night and chase us away.

I was hoping to earn my college degree, but it was not to be because of the length of the major league baseball season. I'd get done in late September, early October, which meant I already would be a month behind in my classes. And I would have to leave for spring training in early February, which meant I would miss the final few months of the spring semester. During my second semester, I met with the dean and asked him how long it would take me to earn my degree at this pace and he said: "Ten years." We both knew that wasn't very practical, so my college career was over shortly after it had begun. I figured it made more sense finding off-season jobs to supplement my income and develop my own business down the road. I never did get that sheepskin, but I did wind up getting a real-life education in business and finance.

I learned first-hand about money matters during my contract negotiations. They were handled a lot differently in those days. There weren't any agents; you did your own negotiations, if you could even call them that. And there wasn't free agency. Major League Baseball had this thing called the "reserve clause," which essentially meant a ball club controlled your rights for life. You weren't free to negotiate with other teams unless you were released. So you essentially had little to no leverage, unless you were a big star, and even then the owners held the upper hand. The only thing a player could do was threaten to hold out, and if you followed through on that you were taking a big, big gamble. There was a salary cap of sorts.

When I joined the Giants in 1954 I remember the owner, Horace Stoneham, telling us that when the payroll reached a million dollars, "That's it—that's all I have." Another huge difference was that there weren't any multi-year or guaranteed contracts in those days. And there was no such thing as a no-trade clause. Owners could deal you to any team they wanted and you had no say. Your only option: Retirement from the game. You were rewarded based on the season you just had. And if it wasn't a good season in the eyes of the owner, you could expect to receive a pay cut.

I received my contract in the mail about a month before I was to report to spring training in Florida and it was for the major league minimum of $5,500. I signed the contract and mailed it back immediately, thrilled again just to be earning a living playing the game I loved.

CHAPTER 3

HOPING FOR AN OPPORTUNITY TO PROVE MYSELF

I HAD GREAT EXPECTATIONS FOR MY SECOND SEASON. I DEFI-
nitely believed I would be used a lot more often and have a shot at
being a spot starter. I had a solid spring, pitching well in several exhibition games, so I was feeling good about my future as we made our
way by train back to Boston for the start of the regular season. Early
that season, we were in Pittsburgh to play the Pirates and this red-
headed catcher whom we had just promoted from Evansville came
running over to me to introduce himself. His name was Del Crandall.
Like me, he was just nineteen years old, so we hit it off immediately.
The team was heading to Beantown for a home stand after the game
and I asked him if he had found a place to live. When he said he
hadn't I told him he could stay with me in the apartment I had, which
was just a couple of hundred yards from Braves Field, our home ballpark. I said, "I'm paying ten dollars a week, so you could pay five dollars and I could pay five dollars and we'll live happily ever after." It
wound up being the start of a lifelong friendship.

On May 1, 1949, I won my first major league start, beating the
New York Giants, 4-2, in the second half of a doubleheader in Boston. I clearly didn't have my best stuff that day as I walked nine and
allowed six hits in eight innings. Three of those walks came in the
top of the ninth when it was obvious that I had completely run out
of gas. But I did manage to pitch my way out of a few jams along the
way, striking out four and inducing the Giants to hit into three double plays. After I loaded the bases to open the ninth, manager Billy

Southworth wisely relieved me with Nelson Potter, who yielded one run before closing the door to preserve the victory. The game actually ended on a double play as Marv Rickert made a spectacular catch in the outfield and then doubled Bill Rigney off second base. After the play, I rushed over to shake hands with Rickert and Potter.

Although I was excited to pick up my first big league victory and was pleased that I gave up just two runs in eight innings and change, I was disappointed with my lack of control. "My fast ball was high and I couldn't get my stuff where I wanted it," I told reporters afterward. "Can't understand it. My change-up works perfectly in practice, but today in the game I couldn't get it over." Southworth was less hard on me than I was on myself. He told the press "Johnny Antonelli did show shakiness in his control, which is the one thing I have been worried about. However, he came through in great style and proved he has the stuff to win against any team when he gets the ball in there. We have been working on his control all along and with more pitching in the games that count, he should develop the ability to get his pitches where he wants them. It was a tough spot for the lad and the outcome pleased me immensely. He'll start and I also won't hesitate to use him in relief if he hasn't a starting assignment in sight. He'll be better next time out. He'll benefit from this game."

As it turned out, I was used sporadically the next several weeks, but little by little I was getting my control under control. On May 25, I suffered my first big league loss as the Cardinals beat me 3-1 in St. Louis on a two-run homer by Stan Musial. I had pitched a lot better in this game than I had in the game in which I beat the Giants, but wound up with the loss. That's the way it works sometimes in this crazy game of baseball. I had struck out Stan the Man on a curve ball that completely fooled him in the third inning. But the Hall of Famer exacted his revenge when he hammered a homer onto the rightfield pavilion roof his next time up against me in the fifth inning. I scattered eight hits and struck out three and walked three while going the distance. After the game, several people, including two Cardinals enshrined in Cooperstown, paid me wonderful compliments. Musial, who would go on to win seven National League batting titles, told the press: "He's going to be a great pitcher." And Dizzy Dean, the last National League pitcher to win thirty games in a season, offered this appraisal: "He looks like he ought to be a great pitcher. He has control and he has plenty on the ball and is the best prospect in many years." Needless to say, their opinions were a major confidence booster. I couldn't wait to take the mound again.

On June 12, it all came together for me as I threw a 2-0 shutout against the Chicago Cubs at Braves Field. That day, Del Crandall and I made baseball history, becoming the youngest battery (catcher and pitcher) to team up for a major league victory. The two of us were a combined thirty-eight years old. I believe that's still the record. You've had younger pitchers win games, but never with a catcher that young. The funny thing is that the Cubs pitcher that game was a guy named Dutch Leonard, who was forty years old. He actually pitched a very solid game, allowing just two runs on six hits. But I had my good stuff going and outdueled him, allowing just four hits and a walk while striking out five.

I worked well with Crandall, who would become one of the top catchers in the National League, making the All-Star team eleven times and winning four Gold Gloves. He liked to talk a lot and he wasn't afraid to express his opinion, even to home plate umpires. When Del first came up, he occasionally would give the man calling balls and strikes a hard time. I finally asked Del to put a cork in it or we'll never get a call.

That shutout was the first of twenty-five I would throw in my career; in fact, roughly one-fifth of my victories would wind up being shutouts, a stat that I'm very proud of. In the next day's papers, there were glowing reviews of my performance that included praise from both my teammates and the Cubs players. Even the home plate umpire, Artie Gore, complimented me, telling the writers how impressed he was with my poise and my tenacity. He especially liked the fact I was willing to throw my curveball in situations where other pitchers would be afraid to. The general consensus was that I was ready to pitch regularly. Unfortunately, my manager, Billy Southworth, didn't seem to be as impressed as they were. He rewarded me by not pitching me again for six weeks.

That really hurt because I felt I was ready to contribute more. I think Southworth was super sensitive about the press coming down on him if I went out and blew a game. Ironically, his decision not to use me resulted in him being blasted by one of the Boston columnists who pointed out that the veteran pitchers were struggling and Southworth has this great, young arm rusting away on the bench. It just didn't make any sense. In hindsight, Southworth's drinking problem may have contributed to my inactivity. He had been hitting the bottle more heavily that season and perhaps that was clouding his judgment because he was making decisions and saying things to us and to the press that didn't make a lot of sense.

My only work—other than batting practice—during that stretch was a start in an exhibition game against the cross-town rival Red Sox. It was at Fenway Park and it was only about thirty-nine degrees. I went the distance that day and experienced the thrill of pitching against Ted Williams, whom I believe is the greatest hitter of all time. I had gotten him out the first two times and when the left-handed slugging pull-hitter came up the third time, we again put on the shift in which we had the shortstop playing on the second base side of the field. I got two strikes on him and threw what I thought was a great pitch. But just before it was about to wind up in Crandall's mitt, Williams swung and blooped a double down the leftfield line. I swear the ball was about two inches from Del's glove when Williams made contact. But that's why he was such a great hitter. Just when you thought you had him beaten, he'd beat you. Later, Crandall told me that just before I delivered that pitch, Williams was pounding the plate with his bat and talking to himself. "I can hit this bleeping kid, I can hit this bleeping kid," he said to himself as he squeezed his Louisville Slugger. What can I say? He was right.

Years later, I faced Williams in an All-Star Game and I struck him out on a pitch where I said, "Oh, no!" the instant it left my hand. I knew it was a lousy pitch—a hanging curve—and I expected Williams to smash it about five hundred feet. But I guess I fooled him because he swung right through it. Hey, sometimes it's better to be lucky than good. To strike out the greatest hitter who ever picked up a bat was a great thrill.

After the All-Star break in 1949, when it was apparent that our struggling ballclub wasn't going to win the pennant, Southworth started using me a bit more. I wound up starting ten games and relieving in twelve others, finishing with a 3-7 record and a 3.56 earned run average. I definitely had some control problems, issuing forty-two walks in ninety-six innings. But I tried to keep things in perspective. I was still just nineteen years old, and I was feeling more and more at home in the big leagues. I had learned an awful lot. I went home following that season optimistic that I'd take a huge step forward in 1950.

You might say my biggest victory in 1949 came off the field because that was the year I met my first wife, Rosemarie. Actually, the story of our meeting began with the final home game of the 1948 season. It was "Fan Appreciation Day" at Braves Field and there were about 38,000 people in the stands. The torn ticket stubs were placed in a huge drum. One ticket was pulled and the winner received an all-expenses-paid, two-week trip to the Braves spring training complex in Bradenton, Florida. Well, my future father-in-law, Anthony Carbone, wound up winning the prize and that next February he and his wife, Margaret, were on the same Florida-bound train as I was. We struck up a conversation. When they told me they were going to Bradenton, I told them I would introduce them to my dad who was already there, and he could help steer them to the good restaurants, etc. And that's what I did. That was the last I saw of the Carbones in Florida. My dad and they really hit off, and that July, when my dad, mother and sister came to Boston to watch me pitch, the Carbones invited all of us over to dinner. I remember telling Dad that they could go, that I was going to dinner to a restaurant with some of my teammates. He informed me otherwise and I wound up going with him.

We get there and I notice this young lady setting the table. Her father introduces me to her. So, we chat and after dinner I'm so smitten with her I even help her do the dishes, prompting my dad to laugh and say, "Geez, you never do the dishes when you are home in Rochester." Rosemarie and I talked some more and my heart sank when she told me she was going out with a Harvard student. I was so disappointed. I thought to myself, "Nothing's ever going to happen for us. I can't compete with a guy from Harvard." But on my way back to my apartment that night, I started thinking differently. I even remember telling Crandall that I just met the girl I'm going to marry. He looked at me like I was crazy. But two years later, Rosemarie and I were married. And you can trace it back to that ticket being pulled out of that tub with the thirty-eight thousand tickets. What are the odds of that happening?

Like most kids, I collected baseball cards growing up. So it was a huge thrill in the summer of 1949 when I received the first card with my picture on it. The card companies—Topps and Bowman back then—would have you sign a contract granting them permission to use your likeness. I think I signed away my rights for something like fifty dollars. Today, players receive tens of thousands of dollars—and sometimes even more for those rights. But it was a different time and you were just overjoyed to know that you were going to be immortalized on a baseball card. In addition to the money, the card companies would send you a complete set of all the major league players from that year. I still get people mailing me cards, and I enjoy seeing them. They certainly bring back a lot of memories. Interestingly, Topps, the leading card manufacturer for decades, has had me sign a bunch of cards in recent years that they've inserted into packs of current cards. That's kind of neat because it introduces me to a new generation of baseball fans. It's always nice to be remembered.

The 1950 season wound up being a big disappointment for me. I actually pitched in two fewer games than I had the year before and made only six starts. I ended up 2-3 with a 5.93 earned run average and gave up eighty-one hits in just fifty-seven innings. Probably my most memorable moment that season occurred on August 31 at Ebbets Field in Brooklyn. I became a part of baseball history when I served up a two-run homer to Gil Hodges in the eighth inning of a 19-3 loss to the Dodgers. It was Gil's fourth homer of the day, tying a major league record for most home runs in a single game. (The record still stands.) I had plenty of company in the misery department that day, as pitching mates' Warren Spahn (second inning), Norman Roy (third inning) and Bob Hall (sixth inning) also were taken deep by the Dodgers slugging first baseman. One of the quirky things about that performance is that Carl Furillo was on base each time Hodges homered.

Four years later, I would be a participant in some more gopher ball history, when, during a doubleheader against the Cardinals in St. Louis, I would serve up two of the five home runs Stan Musial would hit that day. Stan the Man had a good "week" that day, going six-for-eight with five homers and two walks. Interestingly, one of the fans in attendance was eight-year-old Nate Colbert. Many years later, Colbert would become the only other player in major league history to club five homers in a doubleheader.

I also aided Hank Aaron in his quest to surpass Babe Ruth on the all-time home run list. Hammerin' Hank clubbed several homers off me, but I still contend he had some help against me because he had some teammates who were pretty adept at stealing signals so that he knew pitch what was coming before I threw it. I don't say that to diminish Aaron because he was a great hitter with incredibly quick wrists, and you still have to drive the ball out of the park. But it's quite an advantage if a batter knows the pitch ahead of time.

Another superb all-around hitter I faced was Roberto Clemente because he could hit to all fields. If you pitched him outside, he went to right field. If you pitched him inside, he'd pull it. And there also were times when you tried to waste a pitch and he'd line a ball out of the strike zone for a base hit.

Although I gave up my share of home runs in my career, I'd still rather face a big bopper than a guy like Clemente, who had such great bat control and could hit it hard anywhere. People ask me who's the toughest batter I ever faced and I shock them when I tell them it was Johnny Temple. Johnny was an All-Star second baseman for the Cincinnati Reds and a fairly decent hitter with a .283 lifetime batting average. But against me, I swear he must have hit .500. He didn't have much power at all, but, man, could he control that bat. Like Richie Ashburn, the Philadelphia Phillies Hall of Fame centerfielder, Temple had the ability to foul off pitch after pitch, until you gave him one just to his liking. There was one time he must have fouled off about ten straight pitches against me. I walked toward the plate to get another ball from the umpire and I shouted, "Johnny, you're wearing me out. Could you please put a ball in play?"

✪ ✪ ✪

I had entered the 1950 season with my eyes on the fourth spot in the rotation behind Spahn, Johnny Sain and Vernon Bickford, who combined for sixty of our eighty-six victories. I felt even more of a sense of urgency that year because the Korean War had begun and word was that I would be drafted into the army, meaning my big league career would be on hold indefinitely. So, I really wanted to make my mark that season and establish myself as a viable major league player.

But Southworth used me sporadically and I never was able to find a rhythm. I remember thinking to myself: I'm not a ballplayer; I'm a tourist. Southworth said he also had to give two promising minor league pitchers—Normie Roy and Dick Donovan—opportunities. It was obvious that he was still bitter about Perini signing me to a major league contract because he kept harping on the fact that I should have been getting my experience in the farm system rather than in the big leagues.

As it turned out, being drafted into the military proved to be one of the best things that could have happened to me. I was sworn in on March 16, 1951, was assigned to the Third Infantry at Fort Myer, Virginia, and I matured a lot physically and emotionally during my two years of service. Looking back, I tell people that I got my minor league experience pitching in the army. We had a general at our post who was a huge baseball guy. General Herron was his name and he sent out his lieutenants to find the best ballplayers he could because he wanted a good ballclub representing the military district of Washington, D.C. They wound up putting together a pretty darn good team. We had a bunch of professional ballplayers on our club, including Sam Calderone, a third-string catcher with the Giants; Pittsburgh Pirates shortstop Danny O'Connell, Pirates minor league pitcher Bob Purkey; St. Louis Cardinals pitcher Tom Poholsky and me.

Although other base teams seemed loaded with more talent than us, we managed to win the military championship against clubs representing the marines, navy, army and air force. I remember playing against guys like Whitey Ford, Willie Mays, Yogi Berra, Harvey Haddix, Bob Turley and Bobby Brown. And after we won our military title, we wound up playing the Tokyo Giants and the Osaka Tigers in Japan. In my two years playing army ball, I was 42-2, and went the distance in every one of them, throwing forty-four complete games. When I left the Braves to join the Army, my confidence was shaken. I was beginning to wonder if I had what it took to become a major league pitcher. But that experience restored my confidence big time.

Like many of my ball-playing colleagues I didn't see any combat duty. But there were a few occasions when our division came close to being deployed. Our jobs seemed more about boosting morale and providing entertainment for our fellow soldiers. I remember one time, our general granted permission for a magazine photographer to chronicle us going to through military maneuvers. They asked me to toss a grenade through the window of one of our combat training houses. I wound up missing the window with the first throw and had to re-do the scene for the camera. The guys razzed me pretty good about that one. They shouted, "Hey, nice control, Antonelli. We thought you were a big-league pitcher?" It was embarrassing, but we all wound up having a good laugh.

A lot had happened to the Braves in my absence. For starters, when I reported to spring training following my discharge from the army in 1953, we learned that Perini was relocating the team from Boston to Milwaukee because of years of dwindling attendance. In Bradenton, I discovered a pitching rotation vastly different from the one I had left two years earlier. Spahn was still there, in the midst of a string of twenty-win seasons that would earn him induction into the Hall of Fame. But Sain had moved on to the Yankees and Bickford was reaching the end of the road. I quickly noticed that most of the guys from our pennant-winning 1948 club were gone. So was Southworth, who had been replaced as manager by Tommy Holmes, who, in turn, was succeeded by Charlie Grimm. I obviously was looking forward to a fresh start under Grimm. Early in camp, he pulled me aside and told me I was going to be a starter and that he was expecting good things from me that season.

Based on the success I had enjoyed playing military ball, I was expecting a huge year, and the way it began, it appeared my expectations were not only going to be fulfilled, but surpassed. I won nine of my first twelve decisions, and thought that twenty victories—the gold standard for big league pitchers—were within my grasp. But midway through the season I contracted pneumonia. Not only did it force me to miss a few starts, it also left me in a weakened condition for much of the second half of the season. As a result of that and some chronic problems with the index finger on my left hand, I finished the year with a 12-12 won-lost record and a 3.18 earned run average. I still managed to pitch 175 innings—more than I had combined for in my first three seasons—and wound up with eleven complete games and two shutouts. Although I couldn't help but wonder what might have been had I not become ill, I was extremely encouraged by the way I pitched when I was healthy (my ERA was the fifth best in the National League) and by the fact we had pushed the pennant-winning Brooklyn Dodgers for most of the year.

That season also was memorable because we celebrated the birth of our first child, Lisa, in Boston. I was playing in Milwaukee when I got word that Rosemarie had gone into labor and I caught the first plane to Beantown the next morning. Unfortunately, I missed the delivery. When I got to the hospital, the nurses had Lisa in a little shirt with the word, "Braves" written on the front and they had a feather sticking out of her hair. Very cute.

Our second child, Donna, was born in 1956, and I was there for her delivery, but just barely. We were living in Jamaica Estates in northern Manhattan at the time and we had a game in Brooklyn against the Dodgers. I told the parking attendant that I might have to leave early that night because my wife was late in her pregnancy and the guy told me not to worry, that he'd park my car in a place where I could get out quickly. Well, during the game, I receive word that Rosemarie needs me. So, I head out to the lot, only to find my car stuck in the middle. The guy starts moving cars and after about twenty minutes, he finally had cleared an opening for my car and I sped off. I wound up getting back to our apartment complex in time to take Rosemarie to the hospital, where she gave birth about an hour after we arrived.

John, our third child, was born back in Rochester while I was pitching for San Francisco. There were stricter travel restrictions back then about babies flying, so he and Rosemarie couldn't head to California right away. And the way our schedule was, I couldn't get back to the East Coast for about three weeks. That was tough. Regina, our youngest, was born the year I retired, so thankfully there wasn't any scrambling because I wasn't on the road anymore and didn't have to worry about being three thousand miles away from the delivery room.

CHAPTER 4

1954: A SEASON TO REMEMBER

THOUGH THERE HAD BEEN A FEW UNEXPECTED BUMPS IN THE road along the way, there was no doubt in my mind any more that I belonged in the big leagues. I truly believed 1954 was going to be my breakout season. I was looking forward to rewarding Lou Perini for that big bonus he had given me by winning twenty games and helping the Braves win it all.

Unbeknownst to me, during the 1953 World Series, the wheels began turning on a trade that would change the fortunes of my career and that of the New York Giants. The Braves front office believed they were one slugger shy of supplanting the Dodgers. The Giants, meanwhile, had finished way behind the Dodgers and figured if they could add a left-handed pitcher, they might be able to at least make a move toward respectability. Milwaukee general manager John Quinn was targeting Bobby Thomson, but he knew he would have to offer a lot in order to convince Giants owner Horace Stoneham to part with the man who had become a New York sports legend by hitting the famous home run "heard 'round the world" in the 1951 playoffs.

As it turned out, I became the key bargaining chip in the deal. When Stoneham discovered that Quinn was willing to part with a southpaw, he told him: "Give us Antonelli. Give us Antonelli as a starter, and we can go on from there."

Quinn later told reporters that he never wanted to trade me. "I tried like hell to hang on to him," the Braves GM said. "I offered all sorts of other pitching combinations for a deal that would include Thomson, but they weren't interested. I realized after a while that I couldn't swing a Thomson trade unless I included Antonelli. To offer any less would have been an insult to their intelligence. I knew what would happen, of course. Everyone and his brother-in-law would think we were crazy. After all, we'd paid a big bonus to this kid, and we were peddling him just when he figured to be ripe. But we had to have Thomson. At the time, it looked like a pennant if we could get him."

The deal was consummated on February 1, 1954, just two weeks before spring training camps opened. In addition to me, the Braves threw in Don Liddle, Ebba St. Claire, Billy Klaus and a check for $50,000 in exchange for Thomson and backup catcher Sam Calderone.

There had been some rumors about me being trade bait, but I hadn't paid any attention to them because you often saw that stuff written about in the papers, but rarely did they pan out. On the day the deal was struck, Rosemarie and I were running some errands and when we returned to our home in the Boston suburb of Lexington I received a call from a reporter.

"What do you think of the trade?" he asked me.

"What trade?" I asked.

"You've been traded."

"To whom?

"The Giants."

It took me a few minutes to digest it all. Part of me was disappointed because I felt I was just coming into my own and I felt the Braves were on the verge of returning to the World Series. The Giants, meanwhile, had struggled. But the more I thought about it, the more I liked it. I was looking forward to playing for Leo Durocher, a fiery and intelligent manager. Playing in New York City appealed to me, too, because it meant my family and friends wouldn't have to travel as far to see me pitch. I was thinking maybe a fresh start was what I needed at this stage of my career.

The trade was not well received in New York and I understood why. Thomson had been an outstanding player for the Giants for several years and was coming off a season in which he had clubbed twenty-six homers and driven in 106 runs. The writers said the Giants had gotten fleeced in the deal. One columnist wrote that Stoneham, who was known to like his liquor, must have made this deal while half in the bag. (An interesting aside: Thomson would be traded back to the Giants in 1957 and we wound up becoming roommates and good friends. Strange how things work out like that.)

Fortunately for me, Durocher didn't share their views. He seemed genuinely thrilled with the deal because the team was in desperate need of solid pitching. When I arrived at the Giants camp in Phoenix in mid-February, Leo immediately pulled me aside and told me I was going to be his top starter. That made me feel great because it was the first time in my professional career that I was going to be the Number One guy in the rotation. No manager had ever shown that kind of faith in me, and it did wonders for my confidence.

I thanked Leo and told him all I wanted was a chance. "Give me the ball every four days and I'll win my share," I said to him. I wasn't trying to be brash, but I think he could see the fire in my belly. He was a super competitive guy as both a player and manager and I think he liked the fact that I was hungry to prove myself.

It was interesting being in Arizona that February after having spent my first four spring trainings with the Braves in Florida. Today, Phoenix is one huge, sprawling city that stretches on for miles and miles and miles. But back then it was pretty much a little backwater town with just a few hotels. Dan Topping, the famous hotel and resort magnate, had just built one of his first hotels out there, and we used it as our dormitory, so to speak. We'd get dressed there and head to the field, which was nearby.

I didn't get off to a rousing start in camp. In fact, I stunk up the joint my first time out, pitching five lousy innings in an intrasquad game. I was ticked off and immediately asked our pitching coach, Frank Shellenback, what I had done wrong.

"You're overstriding," he said. "Are you too tired to go to the bull-pen and work on it now?"

I said, "Let's go." I was definitely anxious to find a solution. After just a few minutes we had corrected the problem. Frank appreciated my work ethic and afterward told a reporter: "You know what Leo and I like most about him? The fact he was willing to go right to work on top of a five-inning session in that dry Arizona heat. The kid knew something was wrong, and he couldn't wait to correct it."

I appreciated Shelly's comments and his approach. He was very astute at picking up and correcting flaws in a pitcher's mechanics. But he also was a good psychologist, so to speak. He never let me forget that he thought I was a great pitcher. Pretty soon he had me thinking that I was.

In addition to working on my delivery and my psyche, Shelly also helped me perfect my changeup, which became a huge key to the success I was about to enjoy. I'd always had a changeup, but I didn't have much confidence in it. Shelly insisted that I use it more because it would keep batters off balance and make my fastball appear even faster. A changeup is all about deception. You throw it with the same motion as your fastball, but the way you grip it causes it to come in about thirty percent slower. The batter, thinking a fastball is coming, winds up swinging ahead of the pitch. And if he tries to guess it's coming and it's a fastball instead, the ball is in the catcher's mitt by the time the hitter swings. Thanks to Shelly, it became a big part of my repertoire. It got so that I would even throw it in clutch situations, when there were guys on base or I was behind in the count. I would guess that when I was in my prime I wound up throwing it about a third of the time. That's how much confidence I had in it and how effective I was with it. It really made me a complete pitcher. There's no question I would never have realized my potential without it.

I had a pretty good spring training and was looking forward to the real season. But it didn't start out the way I had hoped. I lost the opener, 2-0, to the Phillies in Philadelphia in a rain-shortened game, and in my next start against the hapless Pittsburgh Pirates in the Polo Grounds, I received a huge scare. With two outs and nobody on in the fourth inning, Bob Skinner, a left-handed batter with great potential, hit a wicked line drive back through the box that struck me in the chest just below my heart. It took me several minutes to catch my breath and it made a nasty looking, red, blue and yellow-colored bruise. You could actually see the imprint of the stitches from the ball on my chest for the next several weeks, that's how hard it was struck. But fortunately it looked worse than it felt. After our team physician, Dr. Anthony Palermo, examined me, I was able to stay in the game. I retired the next hitter to get out of the inning and wound up yielding just four harmless hits the rest of the way to secure my first victory as a Giant. They sent me to the hospital for X-rays after the game and fortunately everything was okay.

Pitchers rarely think about it, but you are pretty vulnerable being just sixty feet, six inches away from home plate. And you're actually several feet closer to the batter by the time you release the ball. There's really little time to react because you throw it in there at ninety-five miles per hour and it comes back at you off the bat at about 120 miles per hour. I was blessed because the only other time I was struck, I also escaped pretty much unscathed. A hitter by the name of Clint Conatser hit a shot off the top of my ankle and I yelped as if I had just been hit by a car. I couldn't put any pressure on it and I thought it was broken. They got me into the dugout right away and removed my spikes and sock and put ice on it. The next day I was in pretty good shape and I didn't miss a start.

Of course, some pitchers are never the same after being hit. The most infamous story of a guy whose career was ruined by a line drive involved Herb Score of the Cleveland Indians. He was a great talent—one of the best young pitchers I ever saw—and many thought he would make it to the Hall of Fame; he was that good. But Herb had the misfortune of being nailed by a ball hit by former Yankees infielder Gil McDougald. Score tried coming back from it but was never the same pitcher psychologically. Very sad.

In my next start after being struck by Skinner, I pitched the first of the league-leading six shutouts I would toss that season, beating the Phillies 5-0, and I was on my way.

I took an immediately liking to pitching in the Polo Grounds and wound up having great success there, especially in 1954, when I won my first twelve decisions at the place known as Coogan's Bluff. Like most ballparks of that era, the Polo Grounds had a strange configuration. It was just 258 feet from home plate to the right field foul pole and only 279 feet down the line in left. But it was 483 feet to dead center and roughly 450 feet to the power alleys. It also had a lot of room in foul territory, which pitchers love because pop fouls that would wind up in the stands in other parks would wind up in the gloves of our fielders. For me the pitching strategy at home was simple: Don't let 'em pull the ball. Make 'em hit it to center or right-center or left-center and let the incomparable Willie Mays run it down. Having immediate success at home also helped me win over the fans, who initially viewed me as kind of a villain because I was the main guy in the trade that had sent their hero, Bobby Thomson, to Milwaukee.

As a result of my success at home, I made several appearances on the post-game television show hosted by baseball legend Frankie Frisch. Frankie was one of the ringleaders of those highly entertaining St. Louis Cardinals teams of the early 1930s. They were known as the "Gashouse Gang" because they had quite a cast of characters. Frankie took a liking to me, and although I wasn't keen about being the center of attention, I enjoyed spending time with him and receiving those fifty-dollar restaurant gift certificates each time I appeared. Fifty bucks went a long ways in those days—even in the Big Apple—so I ate well that summer.

I also took a liking that season to having Ray Katt, instead of Wes Westrum, catch my games that season. And if you checked out the numbers you'd understand why. I had a 12-0 record with Ray behind the plate and was only 9-7 when Wes was my battery mate. Don't get me wrong, I liked Wes as a person, but he was a muscle-bound guy, and his legs were so tight that he couldn't squat as low as Ray could, and I liked catchers who could get closer to the ground to catch my low strikes. Ray and I just seemed to work better together.

Mays had an incredible season in 1954, clubbing forty-one homers, driving in 110 runs and batting .345, to win National League MVP honors. Although I never spoke to Willie about this, I've been told by a few people that he may have had something to do with me coming to the Giants. I faced him quite a bit in the army and had a fair amount of success against him and I think he may have told Leo about me. If he did, I'm forever grateful.

We really didn't have much offense beyond the Say Hey Kid and often struggled to win one-run games. One of our big weapons was pinch-hitter Dusty Rhodes, who came up to bat for someone late in the game and invariably drove in the go-ahead run. Dusty was a funny guy, who was always jabbering. We'd go ahead 1-0 in the fourth or fifth inning and he'd come over to me and say, "OK, kid, you got your one run, you better hold 'em." And he meant it. Sometimes, we'd be in a tight game in the sixth or seventh inning, and he'd walk to the rack and grab a bat and tell Durocher: "Hey, Leo, don't you want to win this game? You better get me up there soon." We'd all crack up when he'd do that. But Dusty was serious and supremely confident. He wound up having a great year, with fifteen homers, fifty runs batted in and a .341 batting average in limited time during the regular season. He became a permanent part of baseball lore in that year's World Series with several game-winning hits. And our right-handed pinch-hitter Bobby Hofman also had a great season for us, clubbing eight home runs off the bench. He just wasn't as recognized because he was much less vocal than Dusty.

One of the few times we didn't struggle for runs that season was in a 21-4 pasting of the Pittsburgh Pirates at the Polo Grounds on May 25. It actually was a close game until the latter innings, as we scored five runs in the seventh and eleven runs in the eighth. The win was my sixth of the season, but I also remember that game fondly because I smacked the first home run of my career.

As my league-leading 2.30 earned run average indicated, I didn't yield a lot of runs that season. Most of my twenty-one wins were by one or two runs. During one of my starts, we did have an offensive explosion of sorts, scoring nine runs early. But I guess either I didn't like prosperity or I was in a state of shock because our opponents wound up tying the game and I was sent to the showers by about the fifth inning with no decision.

We had a solid pitching staff. Sal Maglie (14-6 won-lost record; 3.26 earned run average) and Ruben Gomez (17-9; 2.88) were dependable starters and Marv Grissom (10-7 with nineteen saves) and Hoyt Wilhelm (12-4 with seven saves) did a great job out of the bullpen. Wilhelm, who would go on to become the first relief pitcher inducted into the Baseball Hall of Fame, finished with 143 wins—still a record for relievers—and 227 saves. Unlike many knuckleball pitchers, he had great control and didn't walk many. You didn't mind giving the ball up on occasion in the late innings because you figured Wilhelm and Grissom would preserve the win for you.

I made thirty-seven starts that season and went the distance in eighteen of them. That's more complete games than entire rotations have today. Finishing what you started was a big deal back then. A quality start wasn't five or six innings; a quality start was nine innings, and that was my mindset every time I took the mound. No one was better at pitching all nine in my era than Robin Roberts of the Philadelphia Phillies. That guy would never come out of the game. It didn't matter if it were a 1-0 game or a 9-8 game; Robin gave his team its money's worth and wound up with a decision.

I understand the reliance today on closers. But I'm not real keen on bringing in relievers in the fifth inning and using four or five of them every night. No wonder the games drag on forever. Completing games in just over two hours—about an hour less than today's marathons—were the norm in our day. We prided ourselves on working fast. You didn't have batters constantly stepping out of the box, fidgeting with their batting gloves and posing for the television cameras. And you didn't have pitchers standing forever on the rubber before delivering the pitch. One day, I was pitching against Roberts at the Polo Grounds and we took quickly played to a new level. We both had ringside tickets to that night's heavyweight boxing championship bout between Rocky Marciano and Ezzard Charles at Yankee Stadium, which was only a few train stops from the Polo Grounds. Now, we didn't plan it this way, but the game wound up taking just one hour and thirty-one minutes. He won 2-1. We showered, hopped the subway and were in our seats at 10:20, just as the two fighters were about to enter the ring. Again, we didn't plan it that way, but that's how the games were played back then. And I think both the players and the fans liked it better that way as opposed to today's snail-like pace.

I think starting pitchers are coddled way too much these days. There's such an emphasis on pitch counts. A big, strong strapping guy like CC Sabathia of the Yankees reaches one hundred pitches and immediately the announcers are talking like he's going to wither and faint after a few more pitches. Give me a break. I don't know when this became such a big deal. All I know is that we didn't keep track of pitch counts in my day and nobody's arm fell off.

Although I was never into hitting guys, I did believe in pitching inside. My feeling is that the entire plate belongs to you, just as it belongs to the hitter. If you can't pitch inside, batters are going to have a field day against you because they'll be able to fully extend their arms when they're swinging and hit the ball a country mile. But there's a big difference between pitching inside and throwing bean balls. A baseball can be a lethal weapon. I've seen guys get seriously injured and almost killed with pitches to the head.

Probably the worst incident I ever witnessed was a game in Cincinnati when our utility infielder Wayne Terwilliger was hit in the head so hard that it shattered his protective batting helmet as if it were an eggshell. I'll never forget the sound of that pitch from Johnny Klippstein hitting him. It was sickening. I was the first one out of the dugout to come to Wayne's assistance and I thought he was dead because he wasn't moving and there was a bump on his head the size of an orange. They took Wayne off on a stretcher and fortunately he wound up being okay. After we got back to the dugout, one of our coaches said we would retaliate. His exact words: "When Klippstein comes up to bat, somebody better *clip* stein." Again, I didn't believe that bean ball stuff had a place in the game. I think I always had a little fear of hurting somebody. There was this hurler, Johnny Gee, who wound up hitting a batter in the head and was never the same pitcher. I just think the whole thing is childish and dangerous.

I got thrown at only once in my career, and it happened because a pitch I threw to St. Louis Cardinals superstar Stan Musial was a little too inside and wound up hitting him. I wasn't trying to hit him, just brush him back a bit. Well, Eddie Stanky, my former Braves teammate, was managing the Cardinals and he was angry. So, when I came up to bat the next inning I could hear him yell to his pitcher, "Give him one! Give him one!" The guy throws one way inside and just misses hitting me. I tell the Cardinals catcher, "Tell Eddie if this guy hits me he's doing me a favor because I can't hit him." The guy throws another one that nearly hits me, so now I'm steaming. When I got back on the mound, I almost did something really stupid during warmups. I was half-tempted to throw a fastball at Stanky in the dugout, but I refrained. And, in retrospect, I'm glad I did.

I won five of my first seven decisions in 1954, and two of the victories came against my old team, the Braves. I'd be lying if I said I wasn't a little more revved up than usual in those games. I took extra satisfaction in the June 9 win because it came in Milwaukee against Spahn, who, as I mentioned before, had always been cold to me and had convinced Braves' management to trade me. We beat him 4-0, and in addition to tossing a shutout, I also drove in one of the runs with a hit off Warren. In the next day's *New York Times,* one of the writers wrote that, "30,018 disconsolate fans looked on in silence." Yes, it was sweet.

That season the Giants called up a young player named Joe Amalfitano, and I tried to take him under my wing immediately because he had been a "bonus baby" and I didn't want him to go through some of the stuff that I had to back in 1948. There was one time, early on, when a photographer wanted us to pose for a picture together, but when I found out it was for a story about "bonus babies" I politely declined. I didn't want to relive the stuff I'd been through, and I didn't want Joe to be targeted by fans and players after the story appeared. Maybe I was being too protective and sensitive, but that's just the way I felt. I went out of my way to offer Joe words of encouragement. I'd tell him that everything would be okay and that it would just take a little time for him to adjust to major league competition and grow into the job. My hope was that other veterans would see me accepting Joe without bitterness and resentment and they would follow suit. I think it helped because other guys began doing the same thing with Joe and it enabled him to fit in right away and feel more at ease.

That first year in New York, a bunch of us lived in an apartment complex overlooking the Hudson River in Washington Heights, about a five-minute drive from the Polo Grounds. In those days, you played mostly day games, so Sal Maglie, Jim Hearn and I often would carpool together to and from the park. We'd also often drive together if we had a "road" game against the Dodgers in Brooklyn because it wasn't that difficult a drive, depending on the time of day.

Most of our travel to road games in those days was done by train.

You'd have sleeper cars with bunk beds, so you could catch some shut-eye if you were making the eight-hour trip from Pittsburgh to St. Louis, which was the westernmost team in those days. We'd also have our own diner car, which was great because they would feed us on those trips and we were able to pocket our six-dollar per diem for meals.

By the time I joined the Giants, plane travel had become more prevalent. We were the first team to fly charter. There were some harrowing trips in those days, and there were a bunch of guys who were absolutely terrified of flying. Maglie would be so nervous he'd inhale his trademark two martinis before even boarding the plane in hopes it would knock him out and he'd sleep through the flight.

✪ ✪ ✪

One of my biggest baseball thrills occurred in July 1954 when Brooklyn Dodgers manager Walter Alston named me to the National League All-Star squad. I had a league-leading 13-2 won-lost record at the time and was riding an eight-game win streak, so I had a pretty good idea I would be chosen. Despite the lack of suspense, I couldn't help but be overjoyed when I received the news because it fulfilled one of my boyhood dreams and was further validation that I was becoming the star pitcher the scouts thought I could become when I was a teenager. I was in awe when I showed up for the game at Cleveland's Municipal Stadium that July 13. Here I was, getting dressed in the same clubhouse as guys like Jackie Robinson, Stan Musial, Duke Snider, Roy Campanella and our own Willie Mays. I would soon be introduced with them, as well as American League stars like Ted Williams, Mickey Mantle and Whitey Ford, in front of 69,751 spectators in that cavernous ballpark and millions more who would be watching on television nationwide. Pretty heady stuff. Maybe a little too heady, because I didn't pitch that well. Working the fourth and fifth innings, I yielded four hits and three runs—two of the scores coming on a homer by Indians third baseman Al Rosen to tie the score at seven. (Guess, you could say I gave the hometown fans what they wanted.) I was hardly alone as far as getting roughed up that evening. The American League outslugged our squad 11-9 to win a Mid-Summer's Classic that saw records established for most combined runs, hits (thirty-one) and home runs (six) in an All-Star Game. Little did I know I would re-turn to Municipal Stadium a few months later, and this time I would leave a much happier man.

We had arrived at the All-Star break with a 57-26 record that had been fueled by a torrid June in which we won twenty-four of twenty-eight games, a mind-boggling .857 winning percentage. But despite our lofty record, we were still just six games ahead of the Dodgers and baseball history was filled with painful stories of teams collapsing down the stretch. So, we knew we would have to continue to play solid baseball if we wanted to stave off our cross-town rivals for the pennant. And that's what we did. We went a respectable 40-31 the rest of the way and wound up capturing the NL title by a comfortable five games.

On August 30, 1954, my dream season became a little dreamier as I threw a four-hitter to defeat the St. Louis Cardinals, 4-1, at Sports-man's Park and notch my twentieth victory. For as long as they've been keeping statistics, the number twenty has been regarded as a standard of excellence for starting pitchers, so I was thrilled to join that elite club. I also was excited when they told me I was the first Giants pitcher since Carl Hubbell and Cliff Melton in 1937 to reach that milestone. I wanted to keep adding to my victory total in the month of September. Unfortunately, I suffered some tough luck in the final month of the regular season, and lost two of my final three deci-sions. My only win down the stretch occurred on September 13 when I tossed a five-hit shutout against the Cardinals. We won 1-0, and I wound up smashing two hits in three at-bats. I also held the great Stan Musial hitless in three at-bats, not an easy thing to do against a seven-time batting champion and one of the greatest hitters in baseball his-tory. I actually wound up having pretty good success against Stan the Man—until, of course, the game was on the line. I'd wind up getting Musial out the first three times I'd face him and then he would invari-ably beat me with a clutch hit late in the game. The other big thing about that shutout is that it snapped a losing skid and increased our lead over the Dodgers to three and a half games. We seemed to be in control of the race from that point on.

Joe Garagiola, a light-hitting but very good defensive player, wound up catching that milestone win. Joe was a very funny guy, who was always yakking and telling jokes. He grew up in the same St. Louis neighborhood as Yogi Berra, and was actually considered a better prospect than the future Yankees great. But Joe never made it big as a player. He did, however, hit the big time as a broadcaster, providing color commentary on nationally televised baseball games and later serving as a co-host of NBC's "Today Show." That he would go into broadcasting didn't surprise any of us in the least because, like I said, he was always talking to players and umpires. He was a good guy to have on that ballclub. He helped keep us loose in the clubhouse.

CHAPTER 5
A WIN, A SAVE AND A
WORLD SERIES CHAMPIONSHIP

THE PUNDITS ESTABLISHED THE INDIANS AS HEAVY FAVORITES because they had won 111 games to beat out the mighty Yankees, who had won 103 games that season and had been the five-time defending World Series champions. With a pitching rotation boasting future Hall-of-Famers Early Wynn and Bob Lemon—each of whom won twenty-three games that season— Cleveland was expected to have a cakewalk against us.

But we knew better. See, we had played the Indians a lot in spring training because we were among the few teams that trained in Arizona in what they called the Cactus League. We were based in Phoenix and they were situated in Tucson. And we continued to play them when we broke camp and began making our way by train back east. We must have faced each other about eighteen times that spring and we had to win about fourteen of those games. So, we didn't have any fear of them heading into the Series.

I was scheduled to pitch Game Two of the Fall Classic, so I watched the first game from the dugout. That contest, of course, will forever be remembered in baseball lore for the phenomenal running, over-the-shoulder catch Willie Mays made on a blast by Vic Wertz to deep, deep centerfield. Had this been any ballpark but the Polo Grounds that ball would have been long gone. But it was about 480 feet to the centerfield wall there and Wertz had to have hit it at least 460. Although he crushed it, I could tell that Willie was going to track it down because he was pounding his glove while he was sprinting,

51

which is something he'd do when he had a bead on the ball. It was a great catch, but through the years, I saw Willie make several catches better than that one. The thing about this catch is that it happened in the World Series for the world to see. And it wound up gaining even greater stature as the years went on. That first game went ten innings and we won it 5-2 when Dusty Rhodes—Mr. October long before Reggie Jackson claimed the nickname—smacked a three-run, pinch-hit homer.

I started the next day against Early Wynn in front of a crowd of 49,099 that included Perry Como, who was on hand to sing the national anthem. And I didn't waste any time establishing a record that can never be broken, only equaled. I can laugh about it now, but I wasn't laughing when it occurred. The first pitch I threw in a World Series was deposited onto the roof at the Polo Grounds for a home run by Al Smith, a leadoff hitter with as much power as my little sister. One pitch and I'm already down 1-0. I said to myself, "Oh, boy, don't tell me this is going to be one of those days." A friend was in the stands with his movie camera. After I gave up that homer, he put his camera away. Good thing, too, because what followed wasn't exactly a masterpiece on my part.

I was in trouble every single inning that day. But somehow I wriggled out of a jam every time. The Indians got nine hits off me and I walked six guys. But they couldn't capitalize on them, as evidenced by the fact they left thirteen runners on base. I wasn't normally a big strikeout pitcher, but I was that day as I fanned nine, which helped me get out of several jams. The homer to Smith wound up being the only run I yielded in a 3-1 complete game victory. To be honest, I'm surprised Leo Durocher didn't yank me. He could have pulled me several times and I wouldn't have complained because I didn't have command of my stuff. I'm grateful, in hindsight, that he let me work out of all those jams. Sometimes you just don't have it, so you have to rely on guile and grit and grind your way through. All I can say is, thank God they didn't rely on pitch counts in those days or I would have been out of there by the fourth inning. Rhodes came through in the clutch again, smacking a two-run homer in the bottom of the fifth; the guy couldn't have picked a better time to go on a roll. Two innings later, I aided my own cause by driving in a run with a groundout. With few exceptions throughout the history of baseball, pitchers have been poor hitters. I really don't know why that it is, but I suspect part of it has to do with the fact that, when you're a starting pitcher, you only hit every four or five days, so it's hard to develop any type of rhythm. I also believe that you have to focus so intently as a pitcher and you have to exert yourself to the fullest with each throw that it mentally and physically drains you.

I certainly fell into that good-pitch, little-hit category. I had a career batting average of just .178, but I did have a little pop in my bat on occasion. *The Baseball Encyclopedia* credits me with fifteen home runs. (I still insist they shorted me two home runs. Believe me, we pitchers don't forget things like that. I swear it was seventeen, but I may be wrong.) I also had twelve doubles, three triples, thirty-five sacrifices, twenty-six walks, fifty-six runs scored and fifty-nine runs batted in 744 plate appearances. There were several occasions when managers used me as a pinch-hitter and there were times when I also pinch-ran. You'd never see that happen today because if one of those pampered, high-paid starting pitchers wound up getting hurt while batting or running the bases a manager could lose his job. And, of course, with the designated hitter in the American League, pitchers only bat during interleague play, which makes them look even more pathetic at the plate.

With us up two games to none, the Series then switched to Cleveland's Municipal Stadium the following day. There were no off days between Series games the way there are today. We wound up winning that one 6-2 thanks to—you guessed it—more hitting heroics by Rhodes. He delivered a clutch two-run, pinch-hit single and Ruben Gomez and Hoyt Wilhelm combined on a four-hitter. The mighty Indians, whom some had predicted would sweep us, were now on the verge to be swept.

We wound up taking a 7-0 lead in Game Four, but the Indians didn't go quietly. They cut our cushion to three runs and when they got two runners on with just one out in the eighth, Durocher decided to call on me. I can thank our shortstop and captain, Alvin Dark, for the opportunity to pick up the save. A few innings earlier, Alvin told Leo he should consider bringing in a lefthander to finish the game because the sun glare off the centerfield scoreboard was making it difficult for batters to pick up a southpaw's pitches. After that conversation, Durocher approached me and asked if I could give him an inning if needed, and I said sure. So I headed to the bullpen to warm up and I could tell just by the way I was throwing the ball that I had much better command of my pitches than I had two days earlier in my start. Coming into the situation I was, with two guys on and only one out, didn't bother me because—what the heck—I had been forced to pitch my way out of jams virtually every inning in Game Two. The only difference would be that this time I would be pitching my way out of a jam created by someone else. I didn't know about the reflection off the scoreboard when I toed the rubber. All I knew is that I was so much more relaxed than I had been in my start and the ball was coming out of my hand nice and easy.

The first guy I faced was Vic Wertz. He had been giving us a lot of trouble, but I wound up striking him out with a fast curveball on a 1-2 pitch. That calmed me down immediately. I then struck out Wally Westlake to end the inning. In the bottom of the ninth, I walked the leadoff hitter, Sam Dente, but settled down and induced Jim Hegan to pop out to first baseman Whitey Lockman. I then struck out Dave Philley and closed out the game and the World Series by getting pinch-hitter Dale Mitchell to foul out to our third baseman, Hank Thompson. Interestingly, Mitchell also would make the final out for the Brooklyn Dodgers in Don Larsen's perfect game World Series victory for the Yankees two years later. Seconds after Thompson squeezed that foul ball into his glove, I was being hugged and slapped on the back by my euphoric teammates. So many thoughts raced through my mind at that moment. I thought of my dad and mom, and the people I grew up with in Rochester. I thought about the struggles I had endured with the Braves, the times when I questioned if I had what it took to be a big league pitcher and wondered if I would ever get a true opportunity to prove myself. It was mind boggling to me that I had finally reached the top of my profession at age twenty-four. I couldn't help but feel numb.

In the clubhouse afterward, everyone was popping the corks off the Champagne bottles and spraying each other like a bunch of little kids going wild with squirt guns. I tried to put my emotions into words for the reporters. "It's impossible to describe the feeling," I said. "This is the greatest experience of my life. Ever since I was a kid at Jefferson High, I dreamed of experiencing a thrill like this."

What a year it had been. I had been the first southpaw to lead the National League in both won-lost percentage (.750) and earned run average (2.30) in the same season in eighteen years. I had made my first All-Star team, had won twenty games for the first time and had a win and a save in a World Series sweep of a team we weren't supposed to beat, let alone sweep. Plus, I had been named the top pitcher in all of baseball by *The Sporting News,* which was regarded as the bible of baseball at the time. Unfortunately, this was two years before the start of the Cy Young Award, but most agree that if there had been one to give, I would have received it. And back in Milwaukee, Chet Nichols, the lefty the Braves decided to keep over me, went 9-11. I had no worries about receiving a full World Series share this time around. I think I earned it.

We flew back to New York that evening and there was a huge crowd waiting to greet us at LaGuardia. The next morning, Willie Mays and I were asked to appear on "The Dave Garroway Show," which was a big deal back then—the 1950s equivalent of the *Today Show* or *Kelly and Regis.* They filmed Willie and me sitting up in the back seat of a convertible, being driven to the studio, like conquering heroes in a parade. They then brought us inside, where Garroway interviewed us about our World Series triumph. We each wound up receiving an eight hundred dollar appearance fee, which was darn good money in those days, considering I was only making $12,000 a year. A few days later, Carl Hubbell, the Giants Hall-of-Fame pitcher, and I appeared in disguise on the most popular television game show of the time: "What's My Line?" They had me wear a long hoop dress as the character, Molly Pitcher. Carl was dressed in a minuteman uniform from the Revolutionary War. The panel asked us twenty questions as they tried to guess what we did in real life. I remember disguising my voice to make me sound like a woman. It was a lot of fun.

On November 4, 1954, a few weeks after winning the World Series, I returned to Rochester for a day in my honor. My hometown pulled out all the stops. You would have thought I was the president or the pope, for gosh sakes. That's how special they made me feel. And I couldn't have been more touched by their kindness.

The day started with a trip to my alma mater, Jefferson High, where I met with old teachers and coaches and spoke to the students at an assembly. Near the entrance to the school, there was a huge banner spanning two telephone polls that read: NICE GOING, JOHNNY. While we were there, the newspaper photographers took pictures of me sitting at my old homeroom desk. It was a lot of fun and underscored just how far my life had taken me in such a short time.

From there, a police escort guided us to City Hall, where Mayor Samuel Dicker proclaimed it "Johnny Antonelli Day" in Rochester and presented me with this three-foot long wooden key to the city that had been carved and finished by Monroe County Judge Clarence Henry, who was a skilled woodworker.

That evening, my wife, Rosemarie, my parents and my little sister, Anne Marie, attended a huge dinner in my honor at the Seneca Hotel ballroom. It was sponsored by the Rochester Businessmen's Association and other civic groups and more than eight hundred people were on hand, including all the city's movers and shakers and several baseball dignitaries. Each attendee was given a commemorative program that was in the shape of a baseball with a facsimile of my autograph and stitches on the cover. It was a clever idea and contained not only my life story, but also a long, long list of head table guests and a cute menu, featuring such made-up delicacies as "Say Hey Shrimp Cocktail with Willie Mays Sauce."

One of the surprise guests was Lou Perini, the Milwaukee Braves owner who had signed me to my "bonus-baby" contract six years earlier and who had reluctantly traded me to the Giants that spring. I was impressed that Lou agreed to attend because I knew he would have to take a lot of guff from people for dealing me away in a trade that certainly didn't work out for him and the Braves, who had hoped Bobby Thomson would be the big slugger he had been with the Giants. "If I had known Thomson was going to get hurt (he broke his leg while sliding during a spring training game), I never would have let Johnny go," he told the audience. He also recounted a funny story how one of his construction foremen told him, "Boss, you must have had rocks in your head to trade away Antonelli." The Braves owner added that even his young kids razzed him about the trade.

Perini said it was the hardest decision he ever had to make in baseball. But he also seemed genuinely happy that I had finally realized the potential his scouts saw in me. "I was surprised and pleased when I received an invitation to attend the dinner here tonight, which honors the young man whom I admire so much that I cannot put it into words," he told reporters. "Perhaps that sounds a bit overdone, especially since it comes from the man who got rid of him, but it's true. I guess I could talk about Johnny all night. I still feel as if he were one of my own. He never got a big head. That's what counts in this game. He really has become a success story." Perini had become close with my parents through the years. He always raved about my mother's cooking, joking that even if he hadn't succeeded in signing me during his visit to Rochester back in 1948 the trip would have been worthwhile just to eat my mom's lasagna and pasta fazoola. "And I've got to give Gus Antonelli a lot of credit," Perini added. "He is unquestionably the greatest salesman I ever met. And he's also a fine gentleman."

Frank Gannett, owner of the local newspapers and the media empire that would spawn USA Today years later, also had some nice things to say about me, telling the packed ballroom: "No man of fame I have ever known has handled himself better than Johnny."

Near the end of the dinner, they called me up to the podium and presented me with the keys to a brand new Buick. I was absolutely stunned and overwhelmed by their generosity. I've never been one for public speaking. It's funny, but I was more relaxed pitching in front of a hostile crowd of eighty thousand than I was talking in front of a group of supportive people. To this day, I'm still uncomfortable with it. I don't remember exactly what I said that night, but I know I thanked the people several times. And I also announced that Rosemarie and our fourteen-month-old daughter, Lisa, would be moving to Rochester from Lexington, Massachusetts, in the very near future. It just made perfect sense to me, giving the support my hometown had shown me and the fact that I was going to be opening up a business there. They say you can't go home again, but as that night and the years that followed proved, that wasn't true in my case.

The fame I had gained winning twenty-one games and a World Series title opened numerous doors for me. That December it clearly helped me land a job as a spokesperson for the Genesee Brewing Company, which was based in Rochester. Arnie Johnson, who played for the NBA's Rochester Royals, and I would visit distributorships throughout the state and give speeches. Genesee paid us three hundred dollars a week and gave us a company car, which was almost as good a financial package as what I was making with the Giants. Of all the offseason jobs I had, that was the one I probably enjoyed the most.

The fact we had to work jobs when the season was over is hard for people to fathom today. Athletes no longer have to work in the offseason because they make so much money from their salaries and endorsements. But we had to work second and third jobs, and that was okay because I think it kept us grounded and more in tune with the fans because we weren't making a hundred times what the average American was.

I did receive two endorsement deals as a result of my successful 1954 campaign. But, for the life of me, I can't remember how much I made off of them. Must not have been much or I surely would have remembered. One of the deals had me endorsing Chesterfield cigarettes, which was funny because I didn't smoke. In the ads, we worked around that by having me hold up a pack of the cigarettes and say: "Smoke Chesterfields, they satisfy." My other endorsement was for Faultless Athletic Supporters by Johnson & Johnson. That's right, jock straps. They ran a picture of me delivering a pitch for the Giants with the copy about how their jocks provide protection and comfort. My wife, Gail, gets a kick out of it because I don't look very comfortable in the photograph they used.

In addition to working the Genesee Brewing job, I was exploring other business opportunities. I had just received $8,700 for winning the World Series, so I figured the time might be right to put some of that money to work and get something started that would become my second career once I was done playing baseball.

I was approached about opening a Chevy car dealership in Rochester, but when I found out the hours involved —8 in the morning to 9:30 at night—I turned it down. I had spent enough time away from my family during the season and was determined not to be a stranger to my wife and kids in the offseason as well. Shortly after that, a friend told me how he worked a summer job at a Firestone tire store. He said he thought the tire business might be a good opportunity for me, and that's how I wound up getting involved in what would become my second career. Firestone sent one of their vice presidents to Rochester, and we wound up securing a dealership on the corner of Keeler and North Clinton streets with the idea of adding more stores as we went along. I put up about ten thousand dollars and partnered with two other guys, including Bill Calameri, who had been a tire store manager. The vice president agreed that it would be a good idea to take advantage of my newfound fame by calling it Johnny Antonelli's Firestone Tire Company.

I had picked a great time to get into the tire business because in post-World War II America, automobiles were becoming more prevalent and new highways were being constructed throughout the United States. At our peak, we had twenty-eight franchises, which included retail stores, commercial truck stores, retread shops and warehouses. Most of them were located in Rochester, but we also had stores as far south as Binghamton, near the Pennsylvania border, and as far north as Carthage, not far from the Canadian border. I wound up being in the business for nearly forty years. It's funny, but there's probably more people in Rochester who know me as the Tire Man instead of as a former major league baseball player.

I found business to be every bit as competitive as trying to get Stan "The Man" Musial out with the bases loaded. I enjoyed it and really worked at it. I had good supervisors running our individual stores. My big job was landing the commercial accounts, some of them with large companies. It took me several years but I finally worked a deal with Eastman Kodak Company, which was huge. Kodak was a massive company in those days, and had a fleet of about six- to seven hundred trucks and heavy equipment on its grounds. Striking that deal, as well as ones with Xerox, the postal service and the local utilities and phone companies, was as gratifying in a business sense as winning twenty games.

After hearing about my success with the tire stores, Willie Mays came up to me and said, "You're lucky to have your own business." And I said: "Willie, you can be lucky, too. You can have the same business. Why don't I call Firestone and arrange a meeting?" Well, Willie was all for that, so I contacted Firestone and we scheduled a meeting at a hotel conference room in San Francisco. I introduced Willie to the five company representatives, then went downstairs so they could talk in private. The folks from Firestone told Willie about their plans for setting up several stores in the Oakland area using his name. Willie wouldn't have to be involved in the business end of things. All he would have to do is make several store appearances each year to sign autographs and mingle with the customers. Willie seemed genuinely interested until they said that, in a sign of good faith, they would ask him to put up $25,000 as a start-up fee. Willie, who was making $125,000 at the time, was taken aback. "Willie Mays doesn't come up with any money," he said. And that was that. When they came down to the lobby after the two-hour meeting, I asked the Firestone reps how it went and they told me the whole story. It's too bad Willie didn't make the investment because those stores became very profitable, and Willie would have made millions.

CHAPTER 6
WHEN NEW YORK WAS THE CAPITAL OF BASEBALL

THAT WINTER I RECEIVED MY CONTRACT OFFER IN THE MAIL. It was for the same amount I had made the previous season, $12,000. Now, I knew with the year I had, I wasn't going to be making the same salary I had in '54, that this was just a starting point. But I had no idea what to ask for and, as I mentioned before, we didn't have agents in those days; you did the negotiations yourself. I decided to ask our captain, Alvin Dark, for some advice, and he said I should send it back and ask for double my salary. I decided to ask for a few thousand more than that, figuring that the Giants would want to negotiate it down several thousand. I sent it back, asking for $28,000 and to my surprise, our general manager, Chub Feeney, calls me and says, "No problem." I thought to myself, "Man, that was a lot easier than I anticipated. I should have asked for more."

It's funny, but the following year, when I struggled to a 14-16 record, they wanted to cut me way back, but I held my ground. My peak salary would be $42,000 in 1958. A year later, when I won nineteen games, I was hoping to get a raise, but management held fast, and without free agency, you had but two options: Take it or leave it.

People like to ask me what I would be making today if I were in my pitching prime. I wouldn't be pulling down what CC Sabathia or Cliff Lee is making—somewhere in the range of $20 million per year. But I definitely would be making in the millions. Just to show how much things have turned in favor of the players, someone figured out that Sabathia makes more money in one game than I made in my entire career. I don't begrudge guys for getting as much as they can, but I think the pendulum has swung way too far toward the players. Unfortunately, the people who have been hurt the most during this period of incredible salary increases are the poor fans. I can't believe how much it costs to go to a game these days. When I played you could get a bleacher seat at the Polo Grounds for about fifty cents. Now, you have to pay fifty dollars in some ballparks just to sit in the so-called "cheap seats."

To stay in shape in the offseason, I'd go over to the University of Rochester fieldhouse, where I'd run and do some light throwing. I'd grab Dave Ocorr, who was my catcher from that national high school all-star game at the Polo Grounds, or one of the UR baseball players to catch me. That winter throwing helped keep my arm strong and limber and ready to go when I reported to spring training in February.

I'd also work out occasionally with the Rochester Royals. I developed a good relationship with Arnie Johnson, Al Cervi, Bobby Wanzer, Bobby Davies and some of the other players. Sometimes, Les Harrison, the Royals coach and owner, would even let me play in exhibition games to raise money for the local veterans hospitals. I always had enjoyed playing basketball when I was in high school and the military. I remember one time when I was in the army we were playing an exhibition against the North Carolina State junior varsity. All of a sudden, a fan recognized me and bellowed, "Hey, Antonelli, be careful you don't trip over your wallet." I'd hear that kind of razzing from time to time. It took me awhile to shed that "bonus baby" tag, and, believe me, I was happy when I did.

✪ ✪ ✪

I was really blessed to play in New York at a time when the Big Apple was—in documentarian Ken Burns' words —"The Capital of Baseball." The fans of the Giants, Dodgers and Yankees were extremely passionate about their teams and their star players. Their debates were always heated. I saw people almost come to blows while arguing about who was the best centerfielder in New York: Willie Mays, Duke Snider or Mickey Mantle?

It didn't take me long to learn how much our fans hated our

National League rivals in Brooklyn. They enjoyed nothing more than seeing us beat the Dodgers. And Dodgers fans felt the same way about us. The intensity of the rivalry was driven home to me during one of my early starts against the Dodgers in 1954. I was warming up behind home plate at the Polo Grounds before the game and I looked up into the stands and saw these three young women dressed in black with veils. They were taking turns poking a needle into a voodoo doll wearing a Giants uniform. I thought to myself, "Oh, my gosh. I'm in trouble now." I think I lasted about three innings that day.

It was even worse for us at Ebbets Field. Unlike the Polo Grounds, the fans at Ebbets were right on top of you, and you could hear everything that was said to you from the stands. And some of it was pretty harsh, but you took it all in stride.

New York is a great baseball town and I think the fans are the best in the country. They know their baseball. Their grandfathers knew it and they passed it down to their children and grandchildren. When you did well, they praised you, and when you didn't do well, they booed you. And that was fine with me. They were fair. They held you accountable.

Obviously the proximity of the Giants and Dodgers fueled the rivalry, but I think the talent level of those clubs also contributed. I've mentioned the guys we had, led by Mays, who is the best player I've ever seen. But the Dodgers ballclub was loaded, too. Pitching against a lineup that featured Jackie Robinson, Duke Snider, Roy Campanella, Gil Hodges, PeeWee Reese and Carl Furillo was no picnic. And they also had some outstanding pitchers, led by Don Newcombe.

Robinson was always a tough batter to get out because he didn't take a big cut; he made contact. And when he got on base he could wreak havoc with his speed and aggression. He was a threat to steal not only second and third, but also home. He'd get in a pitcher's head for sure. You'd be so worried about him taking off that you would rush your pitches to the plate. He could really disrupt things and change the course of a game.

There was one time, though, where I got the better of him on the bases. I caught him leaning off second base and whirled around and picked him off. But even a pickoff with Robinson wasn't easy because he would get in a rundown and make you really work to get him out.

Years later it was brought to my attention that Jackie mentioned me and the old sidewinder Ewell Blackwell as the two toughest pitchers he ever faced. That's one of the nicest compliments I've ever received. Coming from a fierce competitor like Jackie, I'm honored.

Robinson, of course, will always be remembered for the tremendous courage he exhibited in breaking baseball's color barrier. I was fortunate to play for both the Braves and the Giants, two of the more forward-thinking teams as far as integration was concerned. I was really naïve about segregation when I began my major league career because I had never experienced any of that "blacks-only, whites-only" stuff that was prevalent in the Deep South. I remember running with the pitchers in the outfield in St. Louis before a game one time and looking up into the rightfield bleachers, which were cordoned off. I asked one of our guys what that was about. And he said, "Oh, that's where they allow the black fans to sit." I said, "You got to be kidding me." Again, coming from Rochester, I was just so naïve about that stuff. It was all news to me, and I thought it was so wrong.

When I became a player rep for the Giants in the mid-1950s, I tried to change some of the segregationist policies affecting my black teammates. Teams visiting St. Louis would stay at the Chase Hotel, which eventually allowed black players to room there, but still had a "whites-only" policy for its restaurant. That meant that blacks had to eat in the kitchen and this really ticked me off, so I told the hotel manager that we needed to change this so that all of our players could eat in the dining room. I told him that if the policy wasn't changed the New York Giants would have to consider taking our business to another hotel in town. Fortunately, he relented. It may not have been a huge victory in the grand scheme of things, but at least it was a step in the right direction. It's hard to fathom that such racist policies were in effect not all that long ago. I'm glad that stuff is so far behind us as a country.

Another Dodger legend that I had a chance to play against and get to know was Sandy Koufax. How I met him was kind of funny and speaks to a simpler time. We were getting ready to play Brooklyn in the Polo Grounds when our clubhouse guy came over to my locker and said that Sandy wanted to see me outside in the hallway. I thought that was strange because in those days you didn't fraternize with opposing players, especially before games. I went to meet him, and he said, "Mr. Antonelli, I was wondering if you could do me a favor. I forgot to pack my glove and we don't have any other lefthanders on our team. Do you have one I could use?" I smiled and told him to wait a minute while I went back to my locker to retrieve an extra glove I had. I handed it to him and joked: "You can use this as long as you don't put any bad habits in it." He was scheduled to start that night and I remember his first warmup pitch from the mound missing the catcher's mitt and landing halfway up the screen. Sandy was very wild in those days. But he eventually learned to harness that incredible fastball of his and became one of the most dominating pitchers in baseball history.

I think we bonded because we were highly touted lefties whose careers got off to slow starts. The thing people forget about Sandy is that in addition to that hundred miles per hour fastball, he had one of the nastiest curves you'll ever witness. And if you don't believe me, just ask some of my former Giants teammates. There was one game in the L.A. Coliseum where he struck out eighteen of our guys. I was sitting in the bullpen, watching this masterpiece unfold. Our guys were swinging at pitches in the dirt and pitches eye level. Sandy had his A-game that night, and it didn't hurt that the game was being played in a football stadium where the lighting wasn't so great.

I remember visiting Sandy in the clubhouse on occasion after he pitched. I'd see him in the trainer's room with his left elbow packed in ice. I asked him what that was all about, and he told me that it helped reduce the throbbing from the arthritis he had in his elbow. That he was able to accomplish what he did while pitching in so much pain makes his achievements even more remarkable.

Sandy's dominance on the mound resulted in him being the only athlete to win the prestigious Hickok Belt Award more than once. The solid gold, jewel-encrusted belt was presented annually to the top professional athlete in all of sports at a banquet in Rochester, usually in late January, early February. Well, the second time he won it, a blizzard prevented him from getting into Rochester. I think his plane got as far as Cleveland and it was too treacherous to go any farther, so, at the last minute, he asked me to accept on his behalf, which I was more than honored to do. Just one southpaw helping out another southpaw.

Although Sandy was great, I would have to say the toughest pitcher I went head to head with was Robin Roberts of the Phillies. There were guys with better stuff, but Robin was so smart and so durable. He'd always be out-thinking hitters and you couldn't get him out of the game. He had a rubber arm. The bullpen usually got the day off when Robin was pitching.

Maybe the hardest thrower I ever saw was Herb Score of the Cleveland Indians. Man, could he bring it. And he was just wild enough to prevent batters from ever feeling comfortable at the plate. Nobody dug in against him. I remember our hitters coming back to the dugout after striking out against him just shaking their heads in awe. He had an electric arm. If he hadn't accidentally been hit with that line drive that shortened his career, I think he would have become a Hall of Fame pitcher.

We tend to be enthralled with guys who throw really hard. But I think, in this era of the radar gun, we've become too obsessed with a pitcher's speed. You have so many guys out there who can throw close to hundred miles per hour, but they haven't a clue about how to pitch. I look back at guys like Warren Spahn and Whitey Ford. Neither of them could hit ninety miles per hour on the speed gun, but they knew how to make hitters look foolish. They'd always seem to be one pitch ahead of the batter. The batter would be thinking fastball, and they'd throw a slow curve. Or vice versa. Pitching is about keeping guys off balance, and nobody was better than Spahn at doing that. There's a reason the guy won 363 games. Although he never treated me well, I still give him his due. He's the best lefthanded pitcher of all time in my mind.

As far as stuff and pitching style, I was more like Spahn and Ford than Koufax or Score. My fastball was probably ninety-two, so I wasn't going to go out there like a Koufax or a Nolan Ryan and just blow people away. But I learned to change speeds on my pitches and mix it up pretty good. Once I mastered my changeup, my career really took off. I'd throw my changeup at seventy-five miles per hour and they'd swing way too early. Then, I'd throw my ninety-two miles per hour fastball and they'd be way late on it; it would look like it was a hundred miles per hour to them. It's about changing speeds and location. It's a chess match out there. You're trying to keep the batter off balance. You're trying to outsmart him.

You're also adjusting to the strike zone the umpire is calling that day. I think pitchers have it tougher today because the strike zone has shrunk so much. In my day, it was from the batter's armpits to the knees. These days, it seems like it is three inches above the knees to the belly button. I don't know why or when this tinier strike zone became accepted, but I think it's totally unfair to pitchers, and helps explain, along with the steroids, smaller ballparks and depleted pitching staffs caused by too much expansion, the offensive explosion we've witnessed in baseball over the past twenty years.

The men calling the balls and strikes can definitely impact how you do, and although there's supposed to be a standard strike zone according to the rulebook, it seems its interpretation varies from umpire to umpire. I used to love it when Jocko Conlan was behind the plate because I knew that he would give me the strike calls when I painted the black on either the inside or outside of that eighteen-inch wide plate. He was what we would call a pitcher's umpire. But there were other umpires who would favor the hitters and blow strike calls sometimes on pitches that split the plate in half. There were times when I wanted to ask them when was the last time you had your eyes examined, but I didn't because if you showed an umpire up you'd never get a call your way the rest of the game. I would just grin and bear it and keep my mouth shut, and I think in the long run that helped me. Umpires are human and they have a tougher job than many people realize. Looking back, I think they were fair to me overall, and didn't cost me any games.

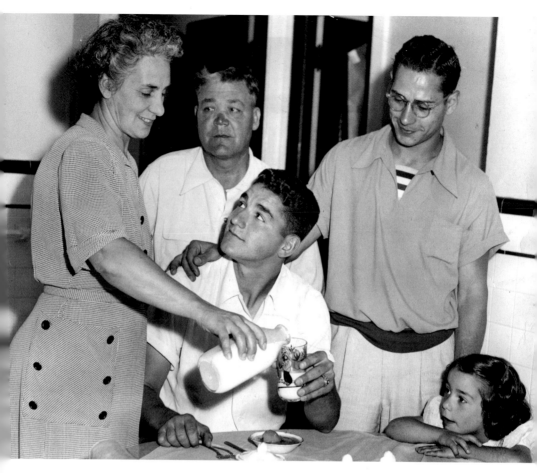

Johnny Antonelli's mother, Josephine, pours him a glass of milk as his father, Gus, older brother, Anthony, and younger sister, Anne Marie, look on at the kitchen table. (Courtesy of Johnny Antonelli)

Antonelli didn't play organized ball until his freshman year at Jefferson High School in Rochester, N.Y. A coach liked the speed of Johnny's throws and quickly converted him from a first baseman into a pitcher. (Courtesy of Johnny Antonelli)

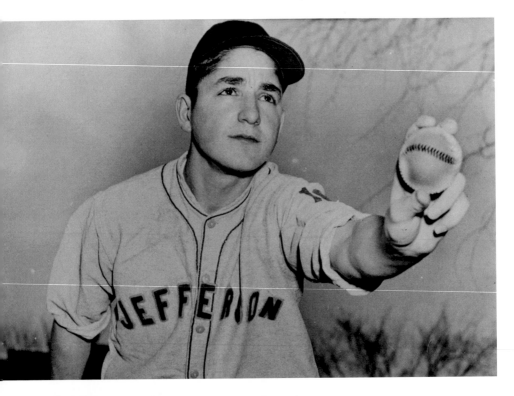

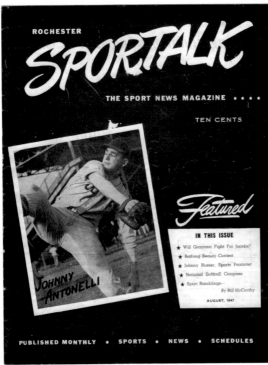

Antonelli was a dominating high school pitcher. In three varsity seasons at Jefferson, he threw three no-hitters, five one-hitters, posted a 15-3 won-lost record and struck out 278 batters in 129 innings.
(Courtesy of Johnny Antonelli)

Antonelli received substantial press coverage throughout his scholastic career, including this local sports magazine story.
(Courtesy of Johnny Antonelli)

Johnny, shown with his Rochester Stars teammate Ray Adamski, threw a no-hitter against the Brockport Barons in a semi-pro exhibition game at Red Wing Stadium — a performance that convinced the major league baseball scouts in attendance that Antonelli deserved a big contract out of high school. (Courtesy of the National Baseball Hall of Fame Library, Cooperstown, N.Y.)

Boston Braves owner Lou Perini and Gus Antonelli look on as Johnny signs a bonus-baby contract for $52,000 on June 29, 1948. (Courtesy of Johnny Antonelli)

Gus Antonelli played a major role in opening the door for Johnny's big-league career. The elder Antonelli would go to spring training with scrapbooks filled with newspaper clippings about his son's achievements and show them to general managers, managers and players in order to drum up interest in Johnny. (Courtesy of Johnny Antonelli)

Antonelli made his major-league debut in relief on July 4, 1948 and yielded a run on a walk and two scratch hits in the eighth inning of a 7-2 loss to the Phillies in Philadelphia. (Courtesy of Johnny Antonelli)

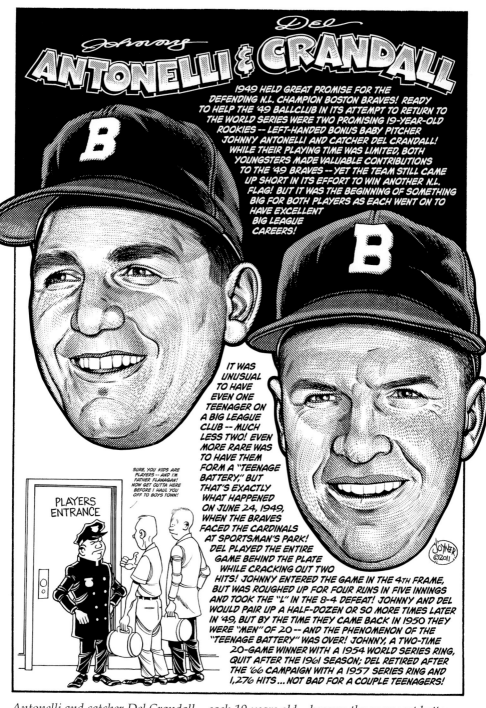

Antonelli and catcher Del Crandall — each 19 years old — became the youngest battery in major league baseball history to combine for a victory during the 1949 season. (Courtesy of artist Ronnie Joyner)

Antonelli and his Boston Braves teammate Sibby Sisti show off the silky uniforms the team wore during night games. (Courtesy of Johnny Antonelli)

In a publicity shot staged by the Army, Antonelli prepares to throw a hand grenade during a training mission. The major league pitcher wound up missing the target and the scene had to be re-shot. (Courtesy of Johnny Antonelli)

Antonelli had a smooth delivery, which is one of the reasons he never suffered any serious arm injuries during his big-league career.
(Courtesy of the National Baseball Hall of Fame Library, Cooperstown, N.Y.)

New York Giants teammates Larry Jansen, Ray Katt, Marv Grissom and Hoyt Wilhelm help Antonelli celebrate his birthday at the Polo Grounds in 1954. (Courtesy of the National Baseball Hall of Fame Library, Cooperstown, N.Y.)

On August 30, 1954, Antonelli defeated the St. Louis Cardinals, 4-1, to notch his 20th victory of the season, becoming the first Giants pitcher in 17 years to reach that milestone. (Courtesy of the National Baseball Hall of Fame Library, Cooperstown, N.Y.)

Antonelli winds up and delivers the pitch that struck out Cleveland Indians shortstop, George Strickland, in the sixth inning of the New York Giants 3-1 victory in Game Two of the 1954 World Series. Antonelli went the distance to pick up the win. (Associated Press)

Antonelli and Willie Mays were the pitching and hitting stars, respectively, of the New York Giants during the team's World Series-winning season in 1954. (Courtesy of Johnny Antonelli)

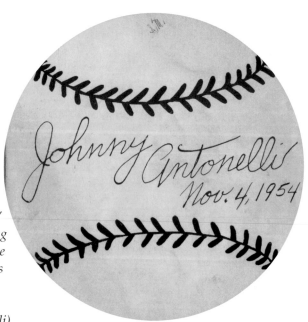

The banquet programs for the "Welcome Home Johnny" dinner in Rochester, following his sterling 1954 season, were made in the shape of baseballs with Antonelli's autograph on the front. (Courtesy of Johnny Antonelli)

During the dinner honoring him following the 1954 season, Antonelli was presented with the key to the city by the mayor of Rochester. (Courtesy of the National Baseball Hall of Fame Library, Cooperstown, N.Y.)

Antonelli finished third in the balloting for the 1954 Hickok Belt Award, which was presented annually to the top professional athlete in the world. His teammate, Willie Mays, edged him out. At the banquet, Antonelli posed with baseball luminaries Roy Campanella, Larry Doby, Phil Rizzuto, Yogi Berra, Mays, Bob Keegan and Wally Moon. (Courtesy of the Ray Hickok Collection)

Antonelli received more national acclaim when he was featured on the cover of
Sport *magazine's June 1955 issue in a photo taken by famed magazine photographer,*
Ozzie Sweet. Sport *was the nation's premier sports magazine in those days.*
(Courtesy of Johnny Antonelli)

Antonelli's family often accompanied him to spring training. This photograph is from the late 1950s and shows Johnny holding son, John. Seated next to him are daughters Lisa and Donna, and his wife, Rosemarie. The Antonellis' fourth child, Regina, was born in 1962, shortly after Johnny retired from baseball.
(Courtesy of Johnny Antonelli.)

Antonelli spent part of the 1961 season with the Cleveland Indians and one of his teammates was Jimmy Piersall, whose struggles with bipolar disorder were well chronicled in a movie titled, Fear Strikes Out, *starring Anthony Perkins. (Courtesy of Johnny Antonelli)*

Although Antonelli had announced his retirement from baseball following the 1961 season, that didn't stop the fledgling New York Mets from sending him a contract for $38,000. Antonelli was flattered, but turned down the offer so he could spend more time with his young family and pursue his tire store business. (Courtesy of the Rochester Democrat and Chronicle)

Antonelli, shown here in one of his Firestone Tire showrooms with manager Joseph De-Paolis, became an incredibly successful businessman after leaving baseball. He invested in his first tire store following the 1954 season. At its peak, Johnny Antonelli Firestone boasted nearly 30 stores and employed close to 300 people.
(Courtesy of Rochester Democrat and Chronicle)

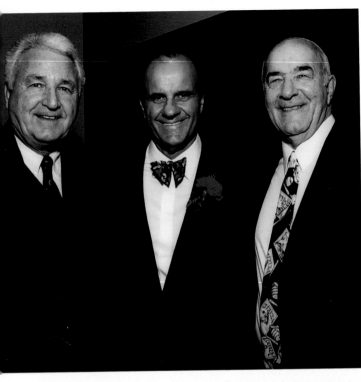

Antonelli posed with New York Yankees manager Joe Torre and former Baltimore Orioles manager Joe Altobelli, at the Rochester Press-Radio Club Children's Charities Day of Champions dinner in spring 2003. Torre grew up following the New York Giants and was a huge fan of Antonelli's. (Courtesy of the Rochester Press-Radio Club)

Antonelli and his wife Gail, watch the Rochester Red Wings play at Frontier Field following Johnny's induction into the Section V Baseball Hall of Fame in 2011. (Photo by Scott Pitoniak)

CHAPTER 7
SOME BIG SEASONS IN THE BIG APPLE

THE 1955 SEASON WOULD BE A HUGE LETDOWN FOR ME AND our ballclub. I wound up finishing with more losses (sixteen) than wins (fourteen) and my earned run average jumped by nearly a run per game to 3.33. I had plenty of company as far teammates having off years, so it was no surprise that we failed to defend our World Series title, finishing in third place, a whopping eighteen and a half games behind the Dodgers, who would finally beat the hated Yankees to win their first World Series title.

My frustrations got the better of me during a September 5 game in Philadelphia, when Leo Durocher sent out our pitching coach to pull me out of a game that I was leading, 3-1. The year before, Leo had allowed me to stay in games and work my way out of jams. But for some reason, he didn't seem to have the same faith in me in '55 and would yank me any time a few men got on base. When Frank Shellenback came out to the mound during that game in Philly, I figured he had noticed some flaw in my mechanics and was going to give me some advice. When he told me that Leo was yanking me, I blew a gasket.

"You've got to be kidding me," I told him. "One pitch could lead to a double-play and I'm out of this jam."

I was really ticked, so instead of giving Shelly the ball I walked over to our shortstop and captain, Alvin Dark, and started venting to him. "Alvin, I'm not going to give him the ball. I'm not leaving this game." I then stomped over to third base and said the same thing to Hank Thompson.

I finally returned to the mound and handed Frank the ball. And as I did, I asked him what Leo had said in the dugout because I definitely was itching for a fight. Known as Leo the Lip, Durocher was a master at getting under people's skin. When one of his pitchers was struggling, you might hear him say something like, "Get him out of there, Shelly, before he kills our infielders." Well, I stormed back to the dugout and headed down the tunnel to the clubhouse where I saw Leo puffing on a cigarette.

"I get paid for winning ballgames," I shouted at him. "I can't win games in the clubhouse. I might as well be in New York than be here."

He was furious with me, and yelled back, "Well, why don't you go back there."

He returned to the dugout to resume managing the game, and I showered, got dressed and headed to the train station, which was just down the block from the ballpark. A few innings after I left the ballpark, Leo had come back into the clubhouse looking for me. When Eddie Logan, our clubhouse attendant, told him I had left, Leo was furious. He called up to the press box and told our public relations guy to tell the writers that I had been suspended.

I didn't know what had happened until my father-in-law showed up at my apartment the next morning with one of the New York tabloids bearing this huge headline: ANTY SUSPENDED. I felt embarrassed, and I didn't know what to do. A few days passed, and I headed to the Polo Grounds because it was my turn to pitch. I knocked sheepishly on Leo's office door and poked my head in.

"What do I have to do to get reinstated?" I asked him.

"Go get dressed," he said. And that was the end of it. I didn't wind up paying a fine, and Leo and I were on good terms again.

The relief I felt from having the incident behind me was obvious in my performance on September 12, 1955. I had a day that would have made Babe Ruth proud. In addition to pitching a complete-game victory against my old team, the Braves, I went four-for-four, rapping a homer, a double and two singles, while driving in four runs. Afterward in the clubhouse, Leo gave me a big bear hug and jokingly told me that I would be batting cleanup the next day.

I know some guys didn't like playing for Leo because he could be quite abrasive. But other than that one incident, I got along with him fine. He was super competitive, absolutely hated to lose. He wound up writing a book titled *Nice Guys Finish Last,* and that pretty much summed up his philosophy. When he retired he was fourth all-time in managerial victories. He would look for any edge he could find to win a ballgame, including getting under an umpire's or an opponent's skin with verbal abuse. Leo was one of the all-time best bench jockeys. Umpires obviously didn't care for Leo the Lip's lip. They ejected him ninety-five times in his career. One opponent Leo tortured regularly was Brooklyn Dodgers ace pitcher Don Newcombe. The minute Newcombe started warming up, Leo would be razzing him, saying derogatory things in hopes of getting Don riled and off his game. And it often worked because Don was a sensitive guy. I actually felt for Newcombe because I know I wouldn't have cared to hear the stuff Leo was jabbering at him. I'm just surprised Newcombe didn't haul off and fire a ball at Leo's head.

I think Durocher respected the fact that I didn't want to come out of games and wanted to battle my way through any adversity I was facing on the mound. I think there were times when I needed to be kicked in the fanny, and Leo was good at knowing when to do that with me and others. But he also realized that those tactics didn't work with every player; that some guys were super sensitive and needed to be coddled and praised in order to get the best out of them. He was a master psychologist and knew how to handle the twenty-five different personalities on a ballclub.

Willie Mays was one guy Leo never criticized—not that there was much to criticize. Willie could do it all: run, throw, catch, hit for average and for power as well as if not better than anyone who ever played the game. Leo treated him like the son who could do no wrong. And that was smart on Leo's part because Willie, besides being super talented, was also super sensitive. He learned early on that Willie would go into a funk if he were reprimanded, so he always treated him with kid gloves.

I remember a time, later on, when Bill Rigney was managing the Giants, and we had a team meeting because the ballclub was foundering. Rigney went around the room, talking about things we needed to do better. At one point, he says: "Willie, you never hit the cutoff man. You have to start doing that." Willie was stung by that and retreated immediately into a shell. I don't think he talked to anybody for two weeks.

Leo, who would wind up being inducted into the Baseball Hall of Fame in 1994, had more star power than most managers, and I think part of that had to do with his marriage to actress, Larraine Day, which helped him become well connected to the Hollywood scene. The Durochers had a house near Los Angeles, and Leo would invite the team to attend parties there when we played exhibition games in Southern California, usually in late March, early April while we were barnstorming our way back east following spring training in Phoenix. There would be people like Frank Sinatra, Gary Cooper, Jimmy Stewart, Doris Day, Ricardo Montalban and Robert Wagner there—a veritable Who's Who of the entertainment industry. It was pretty amazing.

I also remember times when Leo would invite his Hollywood friends to suit up and play ball with us when we were training in Phoenix. One time, I'm pitching in an intrasquad game and Dean Martin is at shortstop and Jerry Lewis is my first baseman. A guy reached base on me, and I look over there and Jerry, in that crazy professor voice of his, is saying, "Come on, Johnny, come on Johnny, throw me the ball, Johnny." I'm bent over in laughter. I toss it easily to him, it gets by him and he takes off like a drunken rabbit. It was hilarious.

Many actors, comedians and singers were huge baseball fans—none more loyal than Jeff Chandler, who absolutely loved our team. In fact, one of his last requests was to be buried with a Giants uniform in his coffin. As player rep, when I received word that he died, I arranged for a uniform to be sent to his family so his final wish could be granted.

I only got to play for Leo for two seasons. He left following our disappointing 1955 campaign over a dispute about the direction of the ballclub. Leo wanted to make some changes, get rid of some of the older guys and give some of the up and coming guys a chance. But our owner, Horace Stoneham, was fiercely loyal to the guys who had won the World Series two years earlier. In hindsight, he was probably too loyal. Leo left for the broadcast booth, where he did color commentary on NBC's "Game of the Week." He later used his Hollywood connections to make cameos on a couple of popular sitcom's, "The Munsters" and "Mr. Ed," whose main character was a talking horse. Leo was a bit of a ham, and I thought he did a good job in front of the camera.

✪   ✪   ✪

Like most people associated with the game of baseball, I was superstitious, but I don't think I took it to the lengths that some guys did. I would never step on the foul lines when I headed on to or off of the diamond. And if I was on a hot streak, as I was during the 1954 season, I would wear the same long-sleeved undershirt, game after game after game—which is why in some of the pictures of me from later that year, you can see my left sleeve looking a little frayed.

Willie Mays had this routine where he had to touch second base on his way out to centerfield each inning. Another Giants teammate, Jim Hearn, had some strange pre-game rituals. If he were scheduled to pitch the next afternoon, he wouldn't sleep with his wife the night before because he believed it would sap his strength. Jim was a nervous fellow, and I remember him coming up to me and Sal Maglie and asking us if we abstained from sleeping with our wives the night before a game we were scheduled to pitch and we told him, "Absolutely not." And he looked at us as if we were the strange ones.

I rarely was nervous leading up to my scheduled starts. In fact, I usually slept like a baby the night before and, unlike some guys with queasy stomachs, I could eat my regular meals on game days. My problems usually occurred after I had finished pitching. I'd be so hyped up, especially if it was a night game that I couldn't get to sleep until three or four in the morning. One time, after I pitched a night game in Pittsburgh, I was so wired I left the hotel and went walking. I remember looking into the store front windows in downtown Pittsburgh at about one or two in the morning when a police cruiser pulled up with its lights on. I immediately identified myself and told them who I was and what I was doing and they asked me if I wanted to hop in the car and join them on their rounds. I said sure. It was a lot of fun and after about an hour they dropped me back at the hotel.

We had curfews on the road, but my managers and coaches knew they never had to worry about me because I didn't drink or carouse. But I had a lot of teammates who did like to paint the town red after a game, and they came up with some pretty creative ways not to get caught and fined for breaking curfew. Some of them would sneak back into the team hotel through the kitchen. Some would actually climb up the emergency ladders in the back alleys. You usually roomed two to a room in those days and I remember one time when I was with the Boston Braves I had to cover for Mike McCormick, a reserve outfielder. A coach knocked on our door and said, "Antonelli." I answered loudly, "Here." And then he bellowed, "McCormick." And I disguised my voice and said, "Here." I don't know if Mike ever wound up getting fined or not, but for most of my career I attempted to get roommates who were content not to break curfew.

Maglie was a great friend; his offseason home in Niagara Falls was about an hour from mine in Rochester and we'd run into each other at postseason banquets. But the man they called the "Barber" because he liked to give batters "close shaves" with the baseball had his quirks, too. Maglie had to have his two martinis after games. I couldn't believe how much he loved that drink, so one time I asked to sniff one of them. I put the glass up to my nose and immediately scrunched up my face in disgust. "How can you drink these?" I asked. "It smells like Aqua Velva."

Perhaps none of the people on those Giants teams was as superstitious as Leo Durocher. We were on a winning streak one time and he refused to allow his uniform to be laundered. And that was saying something because Leo was a clothes hound who always insisted on being impeccably attired, with everything pressed perfectly. But he wasn't about to tempt the baseball gods, so during that win streak he would come in after each game and hang his uniform in the same place. Well, after we had won about eight or nine in a row, our clubhouse guy, Eddie Logan, mistakenly sent out Leo's uniform to be laundered. Leo came in and noticed something different about this uniform he had worn for eight or nine straight games. He wound up going nuts on poor Eddie when he found out what happened. He told Eddie never, ever to mess with his good luck like that again. I can't remember if we lost that day or not, but I do know that every time after that, Eddie made sure he checked with Leo before sending his uniform out to be washed.

✪ ✪ ✪

Now, I mentioned how Leo seemed to have a quick hook with me in 1955, but on May 1 against Cincinnati he was intent on letting me go the distance. In this case, long distance. I wound up pitching sixteen innings, but the way it started I didn't think I was going to last sixteen pitches. The Reds were managed by Birdie Tebbetts, and he thought the best way to pitch to Willie Mays was to knock him down a few times. The strategy incensed Horace Stoneham. So before the game he called Durocher and told him that, "Leo, you need to protect my man, Mays." We have a meeting before the game and Leo says that he's just received a call from the boss and we are going to nip this knocking-down-Mays tactic in the bud. I'm pitching that day and he tells me that I need to send a message to Tebbetts and his hitters that we aren't going to allow this stuff against Willie to go on any more. Interpretation: He wants me to go out and hit a few of the Reds hitters to open the game.

I'm not an advocate of throwing at guys because it means giving up outs and putting runners on base. Plus, a baseball can be a lethal weapon. So it's all kind of foolish if you ask me. But I was forced to follow orders, so the first guy comes up and I drill him right in the back. He goes to first, the second hitter steps in and I hit him in the arm. The third batter comes up and it's Ted Kluszewski, this 6-foot-2, 240-pound mountain of a man with biceps bigger than my thighs. Now, I may be dumb, but I'm not stupid. I value my life, so I wind up pitching to him. As it turned out, I didn't yield a hit the first six innings; Stan Palys finally broke up my no-hit bid with a single off third baseman Hank Thompson's glove. And I gave up just six hits in sixteen innings as we won 2-1 on a sacrifice fly by Bill Taylor. I finished with eleven strikeouts and in the stories in the papers the next day the writers said that my performance was reminiscent of an eighteen-inning shutout the great Carl Hubbell threw against the St. Louis Cardinals twenty-two years earlier. The other thing I remember is that the teams combined for ten double plays to tie a major league record.

I loved pitching in hot weather because your arm felt loose and you could get a good grip on the ball. But there was one time in Cincinnati when the heat almost did me in. It was 104 degrees at Crosley

Field and we were wearing the thick woolen uniforms of the day. Wouldn't you know it, the game wound up going into extra innings and I went the distance as we won it in the eleventh. I lost fourteen pounds of water weight that day. Today, we know how important it is to keep pumping the fluids so you don't get dehydrated. But back in those days they advised against drinking too much water because they were afraid you would cramp up and get a stomachache. Well, we head to the clubhouse after the game and everybody's whooping it up except me. I felt like I was going to die. I kept drinking water from the fountain, but I couldn't stop sweating, so some of the guys helped me into the shower and turned the water on the coldest setting in hopes I would cool down. But it didn't seem to help. They wrapped my head in a cold towel as we bused to the airport for our flight to St. Louis. I continued perspiring all the way there and didn't stop until we reached the team hotel. It's one of the scariest moments I've ever had as a ballplayer. Fortunately, we know better today about the importance of staying hydrated.

On June 29, 1955, I received permission from Leo to return to Rochester to attend the grand opening of my first Firestone dealership on the corner of Keeler and North Clinton streets. We did it up big, offering free autographed souvenirs, free orchids for the ladies and free sodas and balloons for the kids. To publicize the event, we took out full-page ads in the morning and afternoon newspapers. The ad contained a picture of me following through on my pitch with copy reading: "STRIKE THREE! Everybody in Rochester will be OUT to the GRAND OPENING OF JOHNNY ANTONELLI TIRE COM-PANY, Inc., the largest and finest Firestone Dealer in Upstate New York." The turnout was fantastic. We had wall-to-wall people in the store. It made me feel confident that the business was going to be a success, and I truly appreciated the support of my hometown. The people from Rochester have been there for me my entire life.

Among the souvenirs we gave away were copies of the June 1955 issue of *Sport* magazine, which featured me on the cover. *Sport* and *The Sporting News* were the most respected sports sources in sports back in those pre-ESPN, pre-Internet days. They had enormous read-erships, and it was a thrill to be the cover subject on a magazine that highlighted the top athletes of the times. I thought their writer, Al Hirshberg, did a good job with the story. He focused on how I'd overcome the pressures and jealousies of being a bonus baby to become a World Series champion. All these years later, I still get requests to sign the cover. Each time I see that issue of the magazine I'm reminded of that great 1954 season, when everything came together for me.

A few months after my disappointing 1955 campaign, I received my contract offer in the mail. I was not pleased. Chub Feeney wrote me to say that the Giants were cutting my salary by twenty-five percent to $21,000. I told him I didn't think the club was being fair with me. (Heck, today a 14-16 record will get you about $6 million a year.) I asked him what I had to do to get my money back, and he told me, "Winning twenty games again would be nice."

Well, that's what happened. I had a bounce-back season in 1956, going 20-13 with a 2.86 earned run average, fifteen complete games and five shutouts. And I put up those numbers for a team that finished twenty games below .500 and seventh out of eight teams in the National League. When I got into the clubhouse following my twentieth victory there was an envelope on my stool containing a check for $7,000. It was nice to see that Chub was a man of his word.

That also was the season I beat the Dodgers in three different ballparks: Ebbets Field, the Polo Grounds and Jersey City. The Dodgers occasionally would play some regular season games at their Triple-A affiliate's ballpark in Jersey, so that's how that came about. I remember the contest there well because I blanked the Dodgers, 1-0, on a two-hitter in what might be the best game I ever pitched. After Duke Snider singled off me in the second inning, I retired fifteen straight batters. Charlie Neal's eighth-inning double was the only other hit I surrendered. I struck out eleven in the game and gave up just one walk. Mays homered for the only run I needed. I had to be almost perfect that night in front of 26,385 rabid Dodger fans at Roosevelt Stadium because I was going against Don Newcombe, who had pitched shutouts in his three previous games and was riding a nine-game win streak. The Dodgers had a stacked lineup, so it was never easy beating them, let alone shutting them out. In fact, that was the first time a southpaw had blanked them in more than two years.

As I mentioned, some of my fiercest pitching duels came against Robin Roberts of the Phillies. On April 23, 1956, I lost a 3-1 heartbreaker to him in the first game of a doubleheader at old Connie Mack Stadium in Philadelphia. I remember having great stuff that day, limiting the Phillies to just three hits. Unfortunately, I made one bad pitch, and a light hitter by the name of Ted Kazanski made me pay, clubbing a three-run homer. That's the way it goes sometimes in baseball. The margin for error can be miniscule. You can throw a hundred great pitches and just one bad one and get beat. We wound up getting revenge in the nightcap of that twinbill, winning the second game, 9-7, on a three-run homer by Mays in the top of the ninth. Philadelphia fans were always among the toughest to deal with—especially after a doubleheader of boozing—and after Mays' blast they began turning on their own team. When the Phillies came to bat in the bottom of the ninth, the fans started throwing bottles and cans onto the field. Our rightfielder, Whitey Lockman, actually called for time and sprinted to the dugout to get a batting helmet to wear in the field. "I wouldn't mind getting hit by a regular bottle, but when they break off the tops and throw them at you, that's too much," he told reporters afterward. It got so bad that Phillies management called for extra police because they were afraid some of the inebriated fans might charge onto the field.

At the mid-way point of the '56 season, I had a 7-11 record and our ballclub was on its way to a seventh-place finish out of eight teams. I had been pitching well, but not getting much run support. I think my dominance of the Dodgers must have caught the attention of their manager, Walter Alston, because he named me to the National League All-Star squad that would play the American League that July 10 at Griffith Stadium in Washington, D.C. After Warren Spahn opened up the sixth inning of that Mid-Summer's Classic by serving up back-to-back home runs to Ted Williams and Mickey Mantle, Alston sent me in to relieve. I got them out 1-2-3, then pitched my two innings and thought I was through. However, when I got back to the dugout Alston informed me I would be pitching the ninth. I was shocked because the most you ever pitch in an All-Star game is three innings. So, I went back out there and put another zero up on the scoreboard. My final pitching line: four innings, four hits, no runs, no walks and one strike out (Mantle). You can probably count on two hands the number of pitchers who have gone four innings in the All-Star Game. I'm proud to be one of them.

Although they were just exhibition games—and, unlike today, didn't determine which league champion got homefield advantage in the World Series—we took All-Star Games very seriously. This victory marked the sixth time in seven years we had beaten the American League at the Mid-Summer's Classic, and no one was more pleased than National League President Warren Giles. Following the win, he came up to me in the clubhouse and shook my hand several times. "We got 'em again, Johnny," he said, beaming. "This is getting to be a habit and I love it." Alston clearly was happy he had added me to the roster despite my disappointing record. "Antonelli went out there and shut the door in their faces just when it looked like maybe they were going to catch up with us," he told reporters. And Roy Campanella, the Dodgers Hall of Fame catcher, boasted about my live arm. "All he needed was that good fastball today, and he had it," Campy told reporters. "I counted the pitches. He used one curve, a changeup . . . and the rest were fastballs."

After the All-Star Game, our pitching coach, Bucky Walters, came up to me and said he thought I still had a shot at twenty wins. I said, "Bucky, are you crazy? I only have about fifteen starts remaining, so I'd have to win thirteen of them. That's highly unlikely. At this point, I'd be happy to finish with a winning record." Well, he wound up being a prophet. Looking back, I might have pitched even better that summer than I had in '54, because our ballclub wasn't very good. I didn't receive much offensive support and our fielding was shoddy, so there wasn't much margin for error each time I took the mound. But that may have actually helped me because it forced me to focus even more than usual.

At the end of the season, the Giants bleacher bums from the Polo Grounds voted me team MVP and presented me with a three-foot trophy. That meant the world to me because these were the true fans in my mind. Didn't matter how the team was doing (and that season we obviously didn't do very well), they were there every game, sitting in the cheap seats in right field, cheering us on. Through the years, I've given away most of the memorabilia from my career to family and friends.

But there are two things I've kept: the 1954 World Series ring that I still wear and that trophy. That's how much their gesture meant to me.

✪ ✪ ✪

Booze was a big part of society and a big part of baseball during my career. I was a rarity because I neither drank nor smoked. Back then, clubhouses were stocked with beer. I remember after catching both games of a doubleheader, Wes Westrum would drink a twelve-pack of beer before leaving the park and no one would think anything of it. I guess that was his idea of dealing with dehydration because he might lose ten pounds of water weight during one of those twinbills, and he figured those beers would help replenish him.

Our owner, Horace Stoneham, was a big drinker, too, and he liked to invite certain players to join him in his office above the centerfield bleachers in the Polo Grounds. After a Friday night game, he would ask Dusty Rhodes, Hank Thompson, Westrum and a few others to imbibe with him, and they'd wind up drinking the night away.

That could be a problem if we happened to have a day game the following afternoon. I remember one time Thompson was so far gone from his Friday night drink fest with Stoneham, that we had to come to his rescue before a Saturday afternoon game. Hank was too hung over to even walk by himself. We didn't want Durocher to see him in that condition, so we got him dressed in his uniform, wrapped a towel around his neck and carried him out to the dugout, where we plopped him into the corner. He'd literally be sleeping there for about the first six innings of the game. Then, you'd hear Leo yell, "Hank, grab a bat, I need you to pinch-hit." And Hank would jump up as if he had been awaken by an alarm clock, wobble over to the bat rack, grab a piece of lumber, go up to the plate and smack a basehit. Mercifully, Leo would send in a pinch-runner for him, and Hank would wobble back to the dugout and head to the showers.

Not surprisingly, Horace was close friends with New York's most famous saloon-keeper, Toots Shor. Everyone who was anyone drank at Toots' bar. It clearly was the place to be seen. You'd have famous authors, actors, singers, politicians and athletes congregate there. And Toots would be in the middle of everything, holding court with the rich and famous. I never went because, like I said, I didn't drink, but I did meet Toots once and he came across as a big, jovial guy—a gentle giant. One time he invited me, and Johnny Lujack, the Heisman Trophy-winning quarterback from Notre Dame, to lunch at the 21 Club in Manhattan. At the end of the lunch, both Johnny and I reached for the check, and all of a sudden this big hand grabs it. It belonged to Toots. He was the type of guy who was constantly picking up the tab, which may be one of the reasons his bar eventually went out of business. He may have been a little too big-hearted. When Johnny and I got outside, we said to each other, "Did you see that bill?" The lunch had cost something like three hundred dollars, which was big money in the 1950s. I'd occasionally see Toots at our games at the Polo Grounds, as Stoneham's guest. They were such good friends that he made sure the big barkeep was given a 1954 World Series ring along with the players and coaches.

Although I was regarded as a milkshake guy— because that's what I would order instead of booze, that or a soda—I did have one drinking experience. It involved my former teammate and lifelong friend, Bobby Thomson. Interestingly, Bobby had been the main guy in the trade that sent him to the Braves and me to the Giants just before the start of spring training in 1954. The Giants reacquired him in 1957 and the man known as the Flying Scotsman and I hit it off immediately and wound up rooming together. One day, Bobby, me, and Giants utility infielder Eddie Bressoud go to lunch and Bobby says in that thick, Scottish brogue of his, "We're going to have some cocktails." I told him that I didn't drink, plus we had a game that night. But he kept insisting, so I told him, "Order two of what you normally drink. That way if I hate it, it won't go to waste because you can drink it." So, he orders his muddled Old Fashioned, which includes bourbon and vermouth. It's not a drink for the faint-hearted. As we used to say, "It'll put hair on your chest." Well, I took a sip of it and thought I was going to die. Man, was it strong. Somehow, I managed to finish it, but that was it for me. Bobby and Eddie, though, were just getting started. They each have another drink, then order a bottle of cognac. They also ordered cigars that had to be about nine inches long. Now, I didn't smoke either, but they wouldn't take no for an answer, so I took a few puffs on the stogie. Unfortunately, I inhaled. I think I turned several shades of green.

Well, we stumble out of the place and head for the ballpark, not realizing that Giants manager Bill Rigney has called a team meeting. By that point, I was sick to my stomach and thankful I wasn't pitching that night. Rigney posts the starting lineup and the rarely used Bressoud sees he's penciled in at shortstop. Wouldn't you know, even though he's three sheets to the wind, he goes out there and gets three hits and makes a couple of spectacular plays. After the game, Bobby and I ask Eddie where he's going for lunch tomorrow.

"I'm not going to tempt the fates," he says. "I'm going back to the same place and have the exact same food and drink." That cracked us up.

I guess I followed my parents' lead as far as abstinence was concerned. Neither of them drank alcohol, even though we always had it around. Like I said earlier, my dad loved making wine, but he always gave it away to friends and co-workers. And where he came from in Italy, wine was a huge part of the family and cultural experience. It was common for his parents and siblings to have a glass of wine at dinner, even when his siblings were still kids. I wasn't the only one on our team who shied away from liquor. To the best of my knowledge, Willie Mays and Del Crandall also abstained.

✪ ✪ ✪

My trend of good-season-followed-by-not-so-good-season continued in 1957 as I went 12-18 with a 3.77 earned run average. We weren't a very good team and I think the uncertainty over whether we were going to stay in New York or relocate to California weighed heavily on us. Early that season, the Dodgers announced their decision to leave Brooklyn for Los Angeles, but we were kept in the dark about what was going to happen with the Giants. There had been stories that Horace Stoneham was considering a move to the West Coast, but he was always quoted as saying his top desire was to remain in New York City. When the decision came down that July 19 that we would be following the Dodgers to California, I was saddened, but not shocked. I figured major league baseball would want at least two teams out there to cut down a bit on travel. And I knew the Giants were in deep financial trouble because we were drawing flies (average attendance had dwindled to just over nine thousand fans per game) and the Polo Grounds had fallen into disrepair. I obviously had hoped that we would stay in New York because it was close to Rochester, where my family, friends and businesses were. Plus, as a pitcher, I had come to love the Polo Grounds with its spacious foul territory and deep power alleys. The short fences down the lines (258 feet to right field and 279 feet to left) bothered me, but I had learned how to keep batters from pulling the ball, so the park was more friend than foe.

On Sunday, September 29, 1957, I pitched the last game the Giants ever played in the old ballpark on West 155th Street and Eighth Avenue in upper Manhattan. Only 11,606 fans showed up to bid us adieu, meaning about three-quarters of the stadium was empty. Everybody was in a pretty somber mood, like they were attending a wake, which in a way, they were. So many great games had been played there through the years, none greater than the final playoff game of the 1951 season when the Giants won the pennant on Bobby Thomson's home run "heard 'round the world." Some of the newspaper photographers were in a nostalgic mood and they asked Bobby to stand out in left field and point to the place where his home run had landed six years earlier.

Before the game, which came just five days after the Dodgers had played their Brooklyn finale at Ebbets Field, the Giants paraded out a bunch of the team's old legends, including Carl Hubbell, Hal Schumacher, Rube Marquard and Monte Irvin. Jack Doyle, who managed the Giants back in 1895, and Blanche McGraw, widow of Giants Hall of Fame manager John McGraw, also were on hand. In the centerfield bleachers, the fans unveiled a huge banner reading, "STAY, TEAM, STAY." It was, of course, too late for that.

My teammates and I were hoping to give them a victory as a going-away present, but it was not to be. We weren't a very good ballclub anymore, and the visiting Pittsburgh Pirates were stocked with good young players including the great Roberto Clemente. They pounced on me for seven hits and four runs in the first two innings and went on to clobber us 9-1. During the course of the game, the fans went from being melancholy to angry. I had departed for the club-house and my shower long before their mood change. When the final out was recorded at exactly 4:35 that afternoon, my teammates made a beeline for the clubhouse, which was in centerfield. Thousands of fans poured onto the field and began taking the place apart. They dug up home plate and the pitching rubber and tore distance markers and plaques off the outfield walls.

Hundreds of them gathered at the foot of the stairs leading up to the clubhouse, and began chanting, "We want Willie!" They weren't being belligerent. They were just hoping to catch one last glimpse of their hero so they officially could say goodbye. After singing "Auld Lang Syne," they began chanting again. "We want Stoneham! We want Stoneham! With a noose around his neck!" Fortunately, this only lasted for a few minutes, and the crowd dispersed and headed for the exits a final time. Once he was showered and dressed, Thomson walked down the clubhouse steps to the empty ball diamond with his five-year-old daughter and his movie camera in hand. He filmed Nancy running the bases, retracing the steps her dad had taken fol-lowing his famous home run back in 1951. "Just one last waltz around the dance floor," he said, summing up the saddest of days.

CHAPTER 8
CALIFORNIA, HERE I COME

I DIDN'T KNOW MUCH ABOUT SAN FRANCISCO OR SEALS Stadium, the old minor league park we would play in for several years, while Candlestick Park was being built. When I heard we were going to be playing in California, I thought, okay, it will be fun because I enjoy pitching in warm weather. Little did I know how chilly and windy it can be in San Francisco, even in July. I loved the people there; it's a great city, I'd move there tomorrow. And they supported us well, with nearly 1.3 million fans turning out that first season, almost double what we drew in our final season in the Polo Grounds. But looking back, I never really warmed to the weather or that little bandbox of a ballpark. It seemed like the wind was always blowing out there—not a good thing for a pitcher. And it was often cold, which made it difficult as a pitcher to get a comfortable grip on the baseball. Your eyes were always watering and your arm often felt cold and stiff. I remember Willie Mays keeping a handwarmer in his pocket. I still contend that even though Willie wound up having some great seasons on the West Coast, the San Francisco fans never really saw him at his best because of the wind and the cold.

For some reason, the people there didn't embrace Willie the way the New York fans had. He's definitely become a San Francisco icon over time and is now beloved in the "City by the Bay." But it wasn't that way in the years immediately after the move, and that's too bad. I don't know what it was. Maybe they expected Willie to fly through the air like Superman. They actually were more thrilled with Orlando

Cepeda and Willie McCovey. Perhaps they related more to those guys because they were homegrown products. They viewed them as San Francisco Giants, not New York Giants.

I got along well with both Cepeda and McCovey. They were great hitters, and I was just happy they were on my side because I couldn't imagine being a pitcher having to face a lineup that featured them and Mays. Talk about modern day Murderers' Row. I gave both of the newcomers nicknames that stuck. I called Orlando "Chi-Chi," and he liked the name so much, he used it for the restaurant he wound up opening. And after watching McCovey smack a home run and a few other hits to help me win a game, I started calling him "Lovie-Dovey" McCovey, and he loved it.

We didn't have a true union when I played, but we did have player-er reps for each club, and I became the Giants representative after Alvin Dark left the ballclub. You really didn't have much power. You'd try to be a buffer at times when a guy might be having problems with a manager or the front office, but unlike today, there wasn't a strong players' association or collective bargaining agreement in place, so there wasn't a whole heck of a lot you could do. Management pretty much held all the cards.

There was one time, though, when I flexed my muscles as a player rep and invoked power that I probably didn't really have. Just before we were to play our first game in San Francisco in 1958, we had an issue regarding the players' ticket availability. We were scheduled to play our home games the first few years at Seals Stadium, which was a minor league ballpark that held only twenty-three thousand. Eddie Logan, our clubhouse guy, showed me the sheet and it said the club only had eighteen tickets available for the players' wives, friends and relatives, and Willie Mays had already claimed ten of them. Now, I didn't have a problem at all with Willie taking ten of the tickets. The problem I had was the allotment of just eighteen tickets for twenty-five guys. I told Eddie not to worry— I'll take care of this. So, I went to the ticket office and introduced myself to the director and told him that this was ridiculous and that if it wasn't taken care of, we weren't going to play that day. He winds up slamming the door in my face. I was so angry that I began kicking the door. I kicked it so hard that

I thought I had broken my foot. I kept pounding on the door and he finally opened it, and I said, "Did you hear me? I will tell my teammates we aren't taking the field if you don't take care of this problem immediately." Now, the funny thing is that I don't think I had the authority to do that, and management never would have allowed us to stage that strike; they probably would have cut all of us. But the threat of not playing was the first thing that came to my mind. Fortunately, it worked because by the time I returned to the clubhouse, Eddie told me that they had just called him and said everything had been taken care of and we could order as many guest passes as we'd like.

Although I posted decent numbers—a 16-13 won-lost record and a 3.28 earned run average—during my first season in San Francisco, I got myself into trouble with the media after my first start at Seals Stadium on April 26, 1958. After getting our opponents out one-two-three in the first inning, I ran into trouble and wound up suffering the loss to drop to 0-2 on the season. The next day, in one of the papers, a columnist who had never seen me pitch before wrote that I was a "has-been at age 28" and that my fastball had lost its hop and that my curveball didn't have much of a bite. Again, the guy had never seen me pitch before and it was only my second start of the season for San Francisco, so I thought the criticism was rather harsh. Well, I lit into him pretty good when I saw him in the clubhouse the next day. I called him a bush leaguer and told him to get out of the locker room. I made up my mind not to talk to any reporters or pose for pictures.

I was still steaming after I beat the Cubs, 3-1, on a six-hitter in my next start four days later. A photographer from the Associated Press was going to take my picture shaving after the game and I told him to get lost. Later that evening, I settled down and realized how wrong I had been to take out my anger on the photographer and other members of the San Francisco press corps for the actions of one columnist. So, the next day I held a press conference to apologize for my actions, and even posed for a picture with the AP photog. "Of course, I was wrong," I told the assembled media. "Dead wrong. None of you other fellows has given me the needle. I'm sorry as heck and hope you can forgive me. Honest, I'm not a prima donna. If I pitch a poor game I expect you to write it that way. It was terrible for me to take it out on you for the action of one person. I assure you it will never happen again. I never acted this way before and I'm sincerely sorry."

The following morning, in a story headlined, "All's Quiet on Western Front," *San Francisco News* columnist Bucky Walter put everything into perspective. He actually defended me for blowing a gasket after being prematurely judged. He pointed out how I was traditionally a slow starter. But he also took me to task for making it an "all-inclusive beef" with the entire corps of writers and photographers. And I thought he was right to do that. Walter wrote about how I had approached him personally before the game, as I did several other writers and photographers, to apologize. "I greeted his decision, which was at once manful and contrite," wrote Walter. "It was the mark of a young man who could swallow false pride." He ended his column with these three sentences: "Well, the fuss is all over. The scars will heal. And today there's a fine understanding between Johnny and the 'Frisco scribes, even though it came out of storm and fury." Later, I learned that my outburst had prompted St. Louis Cardinals general manager Bing Devine to call Giants GM Chub Feeney to see if I might be available in a trade. Feeney quickly put the kibosh on any trade talks.

On June 22, 1958, I picked up a victory on a day I wasn't scheduled to pitch. Our game with the Phillies at Connie Mack Stadium was tied at four heading into the ninth inning and manager Bill Rigney asked if I could give him an inning or two. I said, sure, and went out there and pitched six shutout innings. We wound up winning the game in the fourteenth on a home run by Willie Kirkland. I yielded just three hits, walked four and struck out seven in the longest relief outing of my career. That season, I led the National League in a category I wish I hadn't: most home runs served up, thirty-one. And I attributed some of my gopher-ball problems to Seals Stadium's pitcher-unfriendly dimensions and the infamous San Francisco wind. That would get me into more trouble with the media—and the fans—the following year.

Despite my problems, the Giants rewarded me with a $42,000 contract offer that winter. It wound up being the most money I made in a single baseball season. (My bonus contract of $52,000 had been split over five seasons: $13,000 that first year, and $10,000 per year for the next four years). I justified the faith the Giants showed in me by posting some of the best numbers of my career in 1959: a 19-10 won-lost record with a 3.10 earned run average and a league-leading four shutouts.

One of the funny moments from that season came in a blowout victory against the Phillies in Philadelphia. I'm throwing a shutout and we're up something like 8-0 when I come to bat in the ninth inning. Valmy Thomas, who was a teammate the previous few seasons, is catching for the Phillies and when I step into the box I say to him, "Valmy, I haven't seen a fastball all night." He said, 'Well, get ready, Johnny because here comes one." I swing so hard I almost come out of my spikes and I foul the pitch back into the stands. "Well, I guess that's it. I won't see another one of those." And, he says, "No here comes another one, right down the pike." I swing with all my might again and the ball sails over the fence for a home run. When I step on the plate, Valmy's rubbing a ball to throw back to the pitcher, and he says, "Don't forget your friends." Wouldn't you know, I get the first two outs in the ninth and up comes Valmy. I'm in a tough spot because I don't want to lose my shutout and yet I feel as if I need to serve up a meatball to repay the favor. I throw about eight straight slow balls and Valmy fouls off each one of them. He finally hits the next pitch off the scoreboard for a double. I get the next batter out, and everybody's happy. I've got my homer and shutout and Valmy ends his day with a two-bagger.

Another high point of that summer occurred on July 7 when I picked up the win in the All-Star Game at Forbes Field in Pittsburgh despite facing just two batters and entering the game when we were down a run. Here's what happened. The American League scored three runs off Pirates ace reliever Elroy Face after he had retired the first two batters in the top of the eighth. National League manager Fred Haney brought me in after Harvey Kuenn's RBI double had put the American League ahead 4-3. There were two on when I entered and I wound up walking pinch-hitter Roy Sievers to load the bases, then induced Sherm Lollar to ground out to Eddie Matthews who touched third base for the force-out that ended the inning. We wound up regaining the lead with two runs in the bottom of the eighth on a run-scoring single by Ken Boyer and a run-scoring triple by Willie

Mays. Haney then sent in Don Elston to close out the game, which he did, and I wound up being awarded the victory. It's funny how things work out. Several years earlier I had been an All-Star Game work-horse with four innings of relief work, picking up the save. And here I wind up facing just two batters and pick up a win. I also was on the roster for the All-Star Game at the Los Angeles Memorial Coliseum a month later, but didn't get into the game. It would be the sixth and last time I would take part in the Mid-Summer Classic festivities, and looking back, I'm grateful to be one of just two pitchers in baseball history to say they had a win and a save in both World Series and All-Star games. (Bruce Sutter is the other).

The way things were going, I thought I had a pretty good shot at reaching the twenty-win milestone for the third time in my career. But those dreams went up in smoke when I blew my stack after dropping a close game in the thick of the pennant race to Don Drysdale and the Dodgers on—you guessed it—a wind-blown home run.

We're playing in Seals Stadium and one of their guys hit an in-field pop-up that just kept going. First, our shortstop, Daryl Spencer, says, "I got it." Then, our leftfielder, Jackie Brandt, starts backing up and says, "I got it." Then the next thing you know, the wind has car-ried the ball over the leftfield wall. After the game, one of the writ-ers asked me what type of pitch I had thrown on the ball that was pummeled. That was the word he used. Pummeled. Well, I went nuts on the guy, and told him if he thought that wind-blown homer was "pummeled" he could take a hike. Now, I had always had a pretty good rapport with the press, especially in Boston and New York. But my relationship with the writers became strained in San Francisco. In hindsight, I probably should have kept my mouth shut, but I had al-ways been a fierce competitor and this had been an especially tough loss to take.

They ripped me pretty good in the papers the next day. I went on the Giants pre-game radio show and apologized for my comments. But that didn't help. One of the writers criticized me because I had made my apology on the radio instead of in the newspapers. After that, the fans really began riding me unmercifully. From the mo-ment I stepped out of the dugout to loosen up until the final out, I heard nothing but boos and profanity. It got so bad that I actually tried changing my uniform number for warm-ups and began playing catch right-handed. It was no use. They saw through my disguise and shouted out things like, "Hey, Antonelli, why don't you go back to Rochester where it snows ten months out of the year."

I finally went to Chub Finney, our general manager, and asked him to come out publicly and back me. Just say I made a mistake popping off, but remind them of all I had done for the organization through the years. He said he couldn't do that because then the fans would be all over him and management. That angered me even more, and I told him he could stick my last two starts. Looking back, that was really foolish on my part. I regret giving up a shot at twenty victories a third time, a feat few pitchers in the history of the game have achieved. And I regret not just letting my pitching do my talking for me.

Of course, even if I had won twenty that season, it probably wouldn't have changed the fans perception of me. They saw me as an anti-San Francisco guy. As it turned out, we blew the pennant by losing eight of our final nine games. We went from holding a two-game lead to finishing in third place with an 83-71 record.

After that latest brouhaha, I could sense that my days in northern California were numbered. My name kept popping up in trade rumors, and I didn't do anything to quell the rumors. In fact, I said publicly that I would welcome a trade back to the East Coast, and following a dreadful 1960 season in which I went 6-7 with a 3.77 earned run average, they accommodated me. I didn't make it all the way back east, but the deal to the Cleveland Indians did put me within a four-hour drive from Rochester and my family. And it would get me away from a place where, sadly, I was being treated like Public Enemy No. 1. The deal was consummated on December 3, 1960, with the Giants sending me and Willie Kirkland to Cleveland in exchange for Harvey Kuenn. It's funny, but just a few weeks before the trade, Yankees slugger Roger Maris had been in town and a reporter asked him about me; he said the Bronx Bombers would love to add a lefthander like me to their staff. But to the best of my knowledge, the teams never discussed a deal involving me. In retrospect, it would have been fun to have suited up for my dad's favorite team.

I was just thirty-one years old and looking forward to reviving my career in the American League, whose hitters I had only faced in World Series and All-Star Games. The Indians— especially their manager Bob Kennedy, who brokered the deal—were counting on me to be a solid starter in hopes of challenging the Yankees and Detroit Tigers for the pennant. But it wasn't to be. I wound up making seven starts and pitching four times in relief, posting a 0-4 record and a 6.56 earned run average. My arm was still healthy, but I don't think my heart was in the game anymore. I had always been a family man, and the excitement of traveling had disappeared long ago. I remember lying on my hotel bed in some strange city at one in the afternoon, staring at the ceiling and wondering why I was still doing this. I could tell the end was near.

One of the few memorable moments I had that summer was pitching in Yankee Stadium for the first time. This was the summer of the great home run chase, when the M&M Boys— Mickey Mantle and Roger Maris—were making their assault on Babe Ruth's single-season home run record. We went into New York for a three-game series and our manager, Jimmy Dykes, asked me if I could start a game and I said, "Sure." I actually had the Yankees beat that day. We were up 3-1 going into the bottom of the eighth, and they loaded the bases. There were two outs and Mickey was coming to the plate. Dykes visited the mound and asked me what I wanted to do. I was thinking to myself: "What a crazy question." I had nowhere to put him and Moose Skowron was on deck, and he was on pace to hit thirty home runs that season. So, it was a case of "pick your poison." I decided to pitch to Mickey and I got two strikes on him. I figured I'd waste one and see if I could get him to go fishing and strike out. Well, I threw a pitch about a foot outside, and he one-armed it to right-centerfield for a bases-clearing triple to put the Yankees up by a run. Skowron then came up and popped out on the first pitch to end the inning. And I'm thinking that maybe Dykes' question wasn't so foolish. Maybe I should have walked Mantle to force in a run and pitch to Skowron. I never expected anybody to be able to hit a waste pitch like that. It just showed you how strong Mickey was, to be able to hit a bad ball—one-handed, no less—that far.

One other memorable moment I had pitching at Yankee Stadium involved my teammate Jimmy Piersall, an outstanding centerfielder who suffered from bipolar disorder. I had just finished my warm-ups and was getting ready to pitch when the homeplate umpire held up his hands. I asked him what was wrong and he pointed to centerfield. "You only got eight players," he said. "You're missing a centerfielder." After a few moments, Piersall emerged from the momuments for Babe Ruth, Lou Gehrig and Miller Huggins that were in the field of play in deep, deep centerfield. Afterwards, Piersall was asked what he'd been doing, and he said, "I was just talking to the Babe." It was a funny line. But there was nothing funny about Piersall's mental illness. His struggles with bipolar disorder were well documented in his autobiography *Fear Strikes Out*, which was made into a movie starring Anthony Perkins.

Although I enjoyed my time with the Indians, I was sorry I didn't do a better job for them. On the Fourth of July, I received a surprise when my old ballclub, the Milwaukee Braves, purchased me in a cash transaction. Seven years after I had left in a trade I was back with the organization that had signed me out of high school, and it felt strange. I wound up pitching just nine games in relief and picked up the 126th and final victory of my big league career along the way, which I guess brought my career full circle because it came—as my first had—in a Braves uniform. My last appearance in a big league game came on September 4, 1961, in a 6-2 loss to the Chicago Cubs at venerable Wrigley Field. I gave up two hits and a run in two innings of relief work, but I also had three strikeouts, so there still was some mustard left on my fastball. There's no doubt in my mind that I could have continued pitching for several more years; heck, I was a lefthander and there's always a need for those. Plus, I had never suffered any major injuries to my pitching arm or shoulder. But I knew deep down that I needed to begin writing the next chapter of my life—a life without baseball. My tire business had really begun to pick up; we had added several stores in the area. But my main reason for leaving was that I wanted to have a more normal life with Rosemarie. We had three small children—Lisa, Donna and John —and were expecting a fourth child, Regina, that April. So the timing was right.

I decided to make my retirement announcement on January 22, 1962, at the Rochester Press-Radio Club Dinner in which Roger Maris would be receiving the Hickok Belt Award as the top professional athlete of the previous year. "I've spent more than a year thinking about this decision," I told people that night. "There are a lot of things that went into it—too much traveling, not enough time with my family. I figure in the last ten years I've been married, I haven't spent more than five with my family. Then, too, I'd like to spend more time developing my business interests. Although baseball has been good to me, I have no desire to be connected with it in any capacity any longer." I felt a great sense of relief and peace with my decision.

I thought that announcement would make my retirement official, but I was notified a month later that the New York Mets, who would begin play in 1962 as a National League expansion team, had purchased the rights to me from the Braves. The Mets actually sent me a contract in the mail for $38,000. But I never sent it back. In fact, I still have the unsigned contract. It would have been interesting to give it one more shot. I would have had the opportunity to become teammates with former Dodger rivals like Duke Snider and Gil Hodges. And the Mets were going to play their first two seasons in the Polo Grounds, which had always been a great ballpark for me to pitch in. So the opportunity was intriguing. If I didn't have my tire business to fall back on, I definitely would have become a Met—and suffered the indignity of playing for a ballclub that would go on to lose a modern-day record 120 games in 1962. And I might have suffered the same fate as Roger Craig, who had the misfortune of losing twenty-three games for the Mets that summer. My decision to turn down the offer prompted a funny response from Casey Stengel, the legendary former Yankees manager who had been tagged to skipper the Mets. He told a reporter: "I guess Johnny Antonelli is doing alright selling those black doughnuts in Rochester."

So, the book was officially closed on my career. I had finished with a 126-110 record, a 3.34 earned run average, twenty-five shutouts, 102 complete games and twenty-one saves. I had led the National League in shutouts twice, had won and saved World Series games and had won and saved All-Star Games. I had played with and against some of the greatest players in the history of the sport and I had played in what many consider the golden era of baseball. Looking back, I have a few misgivings. I'm sorry things didn't work out a little better in San Francisco and I wish I had kept my emotions in check on a few occasions. But, all in all, I can't complain. As one of my favorite singers, Frank Sinatra, once crooned: "Regrets, I've had a few, but, then, again, too few to mention."

That June, I did pull on my old Giants uniform to pitch batting practice at the Polo Grounds. I was on a business trip to New York and my old club happened to be playing the Mets. Giants manager Alvin Dark, my old teammate, asked me to come by and throw a little, which I did. I tossed about fifteen minutes of BP and my arm felt nice and loose. After I was done, Alvin came up to me and said: "Come back and play for us." Then, Horace Stoneham and Chub Feeney greeted me. "I've got a contract for you to sign in my back pocket," Feeney said. I told them I was flattered, but that I really meant it when I said I was retired. It was great seeing them and my old teammates again. Being back at the Polo Grounds brought back many fond memories.

CHAPTER 9

LIFE AFTER BASEBALL

A LOT OF FORMER BALLPLAYERS HAVE A TOUGH TIME LETTING go of the game. And I understand why because baseball is very addicting. That is why so many ex-players go into managing or coaching. I received my share of offers to do just that in the years following my retirement. Both the Milwaukee Brewers and Oakland A's asked me to become their pitching coaches, and a few organizations wondered if I would be interested in managing or coaching in their minor league systems or in becoming a scout. But I really had no interest in that because it meant I would have to hit the road again and be away from my family, and that didn't interest me in the least. I had logged enough miles. I was quite content to be a homebody.

The only times I ever wore my baseball uniform after that were for oldtimers' games that several major league teams would stage. Those were always fun games because they gave you a chance to reunite with old teammates and opponents and swap tall tales about your playing days. Sadly, those games have gone by the wayside. I believe the Yankees are the only team to stage an oldtimers day anymore, and, unlike the past, they no longer invite oldtimers from other teams to play. It's solely former Yankees.

Occasionally, I'd get a call from a friend with a major league team to check out a high school or college pitcher in my area and give them a scouting report. And there were a few times when a coach would ask me to come and help a pitcher with his mechanics. But that was about the extent of my involvement.

I also didn't have any desire to get back into baseball as a part owner, though I did spend several years on the board of directors of Rochester Community Baseball, which runs the Red Wings, who have been a Triple-A affiliate of the St. Louis Cardinals, Baltimore Orioles and Minnesota Twins through the years. To support the Wings and thank our customers, I would sponsor Johnny Antonelli Firestone Tire Nights at old Silver Stadium at 500 Norton Street. We'd give away prizes, like free televisions, airline tickets, etc., to those in attendance. The games were big draws, with crowds in excess of ten thousand the norm.

These days, I'm an honorary board member of RCB, and I still get out to the Wings new downtown ballpark, Frontier Field, occasionally. And each time I do, I make sure I buy a bag of peanuts, just like I did when my dad took me to games when I was a kid.

Since retiring from baseball, I've sometimes been confused with John Antonelli, the former utility infielder with the St. Louis Cardinals and Philadelphia Phillies who later managed in the International League. One time when we both were still playing, Louisville Slugger mistakenly shipped me a case of his bats. I would have kept a few, but he was a lot bigger than I was, so his bats were too heavy for me to swing. I actually met the "other" Antonelli in the 1970s when he was in town managing the Tidewater Tides against the Rochester Red Wings. We posed for pictures and had a few chuckles over our cases of mistaken identity.

I really got into golf after I stopped playing baseball. It became my sport of choice. I actually started playing seriously in the early 1950s. The problem in those days was that you were forbidden by your team from playing during the season because there were fears it would screw up your baseball swing. Early in my career, I joined Locust Hill Country Club, site of a highly popular LPGA tournament in suburban Rochester each summer. I took a couple of lessons and thought it was going to be a breeze hitting a ball that's just lying there as opposed to a baseball coming at you at ninety-five miles per hour. One day, we're playing at Locust Hill and on the sixth hole I must have hit the ball five times and never got to the two hundred-yard marker. I was so frustrated with myself that I broke the club over my leg, put the pieces into my bag and swore I would never play this foolish game again as I stormed toward the clubhouse. By the time my foursome had reached the ninth hole, I had simmered down and resumed play. After a few more rounds, I started to get the hang of it and became pretty decent, once shooting a sixty-nine at Locust Hill.

A few years later, I joined Oak Hill Country Club, which has hosted numerous majors and has been rated the top course in the United States by several respected golf magazines through the years. I eventually lowered my handicap to a six and wound up shooting seventy-one on the championship East Course there. Probably my proudest post-baseball athletic achievement was winning the annual Walter Hagen Cancer Tournament with a seventy-one. That, along with the trophy the fans from the Polo Grounds gave me, are the only two trophies I've kept.

Some have asked me if I thought I might have made it as professional golfer, and my answer is no. I could hit the long ball and I was a pretty steady putter, but my chipping left a lot to be desired. I was content to play in local charity tournaments and recreational rounds with clients. Unfortunately, about twenty years ago, I had to give up golf because I had a cervical problem and it would take me several days to recover each time after I played. I looked into surgery to correct the problem, but backed off because a friend of mine with the same condition had surgery and they inadvertently permanently damaged a nerve in his neck and he wound up losing strength in one of his hands. I didn't want to risk that, so I quit cold turkey. I miss it, but at least I have use of both of my hands.

Unlike many old pitchers, my arms and shoulders are still in good shape. The only time I ever had an arm issue during my big league career was during spring training in 1950 when I tweaked my elbow after throwing the ball too hard while trying to impress my manager. I had a pretty smooth motion when I pitched—I wasn't herky-jerky like a lot of guys—so I think that contributed to my durability. I pulled out my old glove, a Wilson A2002, quite a bit in retirement to play catch with my kids and grandkids, but those days are done because I'm on a blood thinner, which makes me bruise easily. A few catches and my hand is completely black and blue.

The thing I valued most after retiring from baseball was spending more time with my wife and our kids. Nightly family dinners were a big part of my youth and it became a tradition Rosemarie and I tried to continue when we became parents. Looking back, one of the things I'm most proud of is that each of my kids graduated from college. Lisa went on to teach elementary school. Donna became a nurse. John took over our tire business and after we sold it, he became an executive with Starbucks Coffee Company, helping establish numerous franchises in Germany and other parts of Europe. And Regina, a drama major, pursued an acting career. The four of them provided us with a dozen grandchildren and four great-grandchildren. They keep us busy.

My wife, Rosemarie, was a fabulous wife, mother and grandmother. Her death in 2002 hit me like a ton of bricks. She had battled cancer off and on for nearly sixteen years. We'd been married for fifty-one years and had shared so many wonderful times together. Her passing was the most difficult thing I've ever had to deal with. I was a wreck for a while. Fortunately my kids and friends were there for me. Somebody was always checking in on me, dragging me out for lunch or dinner or a cup of coffee.

Never in a million years did I expect to get married again, but sometimes life throws you a curve and you hit it out of the park. After several years of being a hermit, I was blessed to meet and fall in love with another great woman, Gail. She, too, had lost her spouse, and my friends and I would see her and her friends at the Charbroil Family Restaurant, a popular diner in suburban Rochester where everyone and his brother seems to go for breakfast and lunch. We became friends and I eventually asked her out for a date, and the rest, as they say, is history. We got married in 2006 and we—along with our Standard Schnauzer, Topper—couldn't be happier, splitting time between our homes in Rochester and Santa Fe, New Mexico. Gail has a great sense of humor. She likes to joke, "I also had no intention of getting married again, but John says he chased me until I caught him."

Once I got out of baseball, I was able to really grow my business. As I mentioned, at our peak, we had twenty-eight stores and nearly three hundred fulltime employees. We were really big into delivering quality customer service and I think that helped our business boom.

One of our promotional services involved a truck we'd send out during morning rush hour traffic called "Captain Friendly." These were the days before cell phones, so if someone had a car-related program, the crew from the "Captain Friendly" truck would stop and assist with putting on a spare tire or charging someone's dead battery, etc. One day I received this wonderful letter from a lady who had been assisted by our crew. It read:

Dear Mr. Antonelli:
I was on my way to work and I had a flat tire. So I pulled over to the side of the road and parked there for a few minutes and, lo and behold, I saw this flashing light and it was Captain Friendly. He fixed my tire and I was able to make it to work on time. I was so happy that I went right to Goodyear the next day and bought four tires.

Thank you so much.
Miss So-and-So

It was a lovely letter. Just one problem—we sold Firestone, not Goodyear, tires. So I wrote her back and thanked her for the kind letter and asked her to think of Firestones the next time she was in need of tires. I did get a chuckle out of it, but as a businessman you worry about people confusing your brand with another.

I had often dreamed of getting into the restaurant business and that dream came true when I purchased the Clintonaire Restaurant. We lined up some pretty good people and the food was excellent, but our timing proved to be horrible. The restaurant was located in downtown Rochester right next to Xerox Tower, which, at the time, was the document company's world headquarters. Great location, but we had the misfortune of opening at a time when they were doing massive construction near the tower and our restaurant—construction that lasted over a year. It killed business and I wound up selling the place. Too bad, too, because we had done everything right and I think it would have taken off otherwise.

I continue to watch a lot of baseball. The game will always be in my blood. Today's players are very talented and, of course, bigger than ever. Being a former pitcher, I tend to pitch the game in my head while watching the pitcher on the television. I'll think about what I would throw certain guys and critique the pitchers. Over the past ten to fifteen years, I've enjoyed watching pitchers like Greg Maddux. He probably couldn't break a pane of glass with his fastball. But he could definitely outsmart you and make you look silly. In my mind, he's the epitome of what a pitcher should be. I really respect a guy like New York Yankees reliever Mariano Rivera. He has impeccable control, and he is so smooth. I take my hat off to him.

I definitely have a number of opinions about the modern game. Like I said earlier, I hate the plodding pace of today's games. Too many pitching changes. Too much stepping out of the batter's box. Too much time waiting for a guy to deliver the pitch. Maybe it's because I'm a National League guy at heart, and maybe it's because I was a pitcher who liked to take my turn at bat. But for some reason I don't like the designated hitter. I know people love offense, but it really does take so much strategy out of the game.

Without question, the use of performance-enhancing drugs has hurt the game. It gave the users too much of an advantage. I don't believe any of the people who used steroids belong in the Hall of Fame. I know that might sound harsh, but it's the way I feel. I'm not saying that everybody from my era would have abstained from using them had they been available. Some no doubt would have used them in hopes of finding an edge. And if they had, they would have had to pay the consequences, just as these guys are going to have to.

I get asked a lot about whether Pete Rose belongs in the Hall of Fame after violating the rule that prohibits you from gambling on games. I've mellowed a bit on this issue as I've grown older. The thing, though, that really bothers me is how Pete lied when it first happened and continued to be adamant about his innocence before finally owing up to it. I'd probably still keep him banished, but I'm willing to listen to arguments for the ban to be lifted.

I obviously try to follow my former teams, especially the Giants, but it's tough because I usually fall asleep before those West Coast games start. I was ecstatic when they won it all in 2010. Because it was the franchise's first World Series title since we won it all in 1954, I received several phone calls from sportswriters asking me to reminisce. During the decisive game in the Series, they showed an old film clip of me so people would know how long it had been since the Giants had won the Fall Classic. That was a thrill that caught me totally off-guard.

The organization has been really good to me and my teammates, flying us to San Francisco for special events in recent years. Their new ballpark down near the Fisherman's Wharf is gorgeous, and ballclub management and the fans have greeted us with open arms. The only disappointing thing during those visits was the attitude of some of the modern-day players. Barry Bonds acted like a jerk to us. He had this couldn't-be-bothered attitude, and that's too bad. He and his teammates didn't embrace us the way you see the current Yankees embrace the past on Oldtimers' Day.

Although I threw my last pitch a half century ago and haven't been in the tire business for nearly two decades, my hometown continues to be very good to me. I was named to the inaugural class of the Frontier Field Walk of Fame in 1997 and last summer I was part of the first class to be inducted into the Section V (Rochester area) Baseball Hall of Fame. There were nine inductees overall, including former big-leaguers Bob Keegan, George Selkirk, Mike Jones, Dave Giusti and Howie Krist. It was an honor, and it also reminded me of what a rich baseball tradition my hometown has.

In 2004, in commemoration of the fiftieth anniversary of the Giants World Series championship, I was honored with the Casey Stengel "You Could Look It Up" Award from the New York chapter of the Baseball Writers Association of America. That was a lot of fun and I got to renew some old acquaintances. It meant a lot to me that Bobby Thomson, my old roommate, introduced me at the banquet. I also got see Gil Hodges' widow, who had me and the audience in stitches when she thanked me for having served up Gil's record-tying fourth home run in a single game many years before.

I still receive autograph requests in the mail and I'm more than happy to sign the cards, pictures and other memorabilia I receive. I don't charge and on the rare occasions when I do a show, if I get money from a promoter I donate it all to a charity like the American Cancer Society in memory of my late wife.

One request that really touched me was from a guy named Mark Seager a few years ago. Mark's dad, Larry Seager, had attended Jefferson High several years after I did, and he remembered my visit to the school following my championship season in 1954. Larry was a freshman at the time and the photographers asked him to move so they could snap pictures of me sitting at my old homeroom desk. I guess from that time on, Larry became a big fan of mine, collecting every card, photograph and piece of memorabilia from my baseball career. Well, all these years later, I received a letter from his son telling me that Larry had been diagnosed with cancer. His family was going to hold a surprise seventieth birthday party for him at Red Fedele's Brook House, a popular Rochester restaurant. He even offered to send a limo to pick me up if I would attend. I told him that wasn't necessary and that we'd be happy to participate.

The look on Larry's face when I walked in was priceless. He looked and acted like a guy who was about to turn seven rather than seventy. I chatted, posed for pictures and gave him an autographed baseball. That ball was from one of my 126 big league victories.

Not long after that we received a wonderful thank you letter from his son. It read, in part:

Johnny,
I wanted to let a few days pass before I sat down to write a letter of thanks to you. I wanted to let the events and emotions of January 17th settle in my mind.

That night, after his party, my father and I were sitting alone at the table drinking coffee, and talking about—well—you. My dad sat there, with the ball in his hand smiling. He looked up and said, "Boy, that was really something, wasn't it?"'

It sure was.

You are a gentleman, Mr. Antonelli. I think what is most remarkable about you, at least to what my eyes had seen in the time I spent with you, is your humility. Let's face it, you were an MLB All-Star pitcher for several years of your life and a very successful businessman. It is clear, probably on an almost daily basis, you still have men and women walk up to you with "that look" in their eyes of adoration and appreciation. Yet there isn't a hint of egotism about you. How you have not let your success and local/national celebrity go to your head is a testament to your character.

You really made me look good that Sunday evening; I thank you for that. You touched my father very deeply with what you did for him. As we sat at the coffee table that evening, he started to cry. He would probably be a bit upset if he knew I shared that with you, but he did. He didn't say anything as he cried but I knew that it had to do with the previous few hours of family and friends—your gift, and with the fact that you were there; that you went out of your way to be there for HIS birthday.

When my parents moved back to Rochester from Phoenix last year, my father planned to finish the basement in their new home and create a den for himself similar to his den in Phoenix, where he displayed all his collectibles. My father collects many things—Genesee Beer collectibles, vintage trains, Sinatra memorabilia and, of course, Johnny Antonelli memorabilia (you're in good company). After he was diagnosed with cancer, he wanted to put the construction of the den on hold. "You know, just in case," he would say. Well, the morning after his party, he woke up and informed us all at the breakfast table that he was going to call the construction company and have them go ahead with the completion of his den. There is absolutely no doubt in my mind that your presence at his party, your gift, and the uplifting experience you gave to him had something to do with his decision to do this for himself, to not let his illness keep him from those things he would do otherwise.

I have brought much away from this trip to New York in the form of life lessons; the most important of which is the inherent ability of one person to bring complete joy to another through one simple act of kindness and generosity.

Thank you again, Johnny. You have a wonderful spirit about you.

Yours,
Mark Seager

Mark's letter brought tears to my eyes. It reminded me how much an athlete can touch people and why I've always tried to be accommodating and cordial to fans because just a little act of kindness can make a big impact on somebody.

Looking back, I realize how blessed I've been. I owe so much to baseball, my family, my friends and my hometown, which has always been good to me—still is. I've had the opportunity to live a life where my dreams came true. It's been a truly memorable ride.

JOHNNY ANTONELLI'S YEAR-BY-YEAR STATISTICS

JOHNNY AUGUST ANTONELLI
POSITION: Pitcher
HEIGHT: 6′ 1″
WEIGHT: 185
BATS: Left
THROWS: Left
BORN: April 12, 1930 in Rochester, New York
HIGH SCHOOL: Jefferson (Rochester, New York)
SIGNED BY the Boston Braves of the National League as an amateur
free agent in June 1948 for a bonus of $52,000
MAJOR LEAGUE DEBUT: July 4, 1948
FINAL GAME: September 4, 1961
TEAMS: Boston and Milwaukee Braves; New York and San Francisco
Giants, and Cleveland Indians.
JERSEY NUMBERS: 34, 43, 23

PITCHING STATS

Year	Age	Team	G	GS	GF	W	L	PCT	ERA	CG	SHO	SV	IP	BF	H	ER	R	HR	BB	IBB	SO	WP	HBP	BK	HLD
1948	18	Braves	4	0	4	0	0	.000	2.25	0	0	1	4.0	17	2	1	1	0	3	–	0	0	0	0	–
1949	19	Braves	22	10	6	3	7	.300	3.56	3	1	0	96.0	416	99	38	49	6	42	–	48	3	2	0	–
1950	20	Braves	20	6	6	2	3	.400	5.93	2	1	0	57.2	275	81	38	46	3	22	–	33	0	4	1	–
1953	23	Braves	31	26	2	12	12	.500	3.18	11	2	1	175.1	763	167	62	83	15	71	–	131	3	1	0	–
1954	24	Giants	39	37	2	21	7	.750	2.30	18	6	2	258.2	1,071	209	66	78	22	94	–	152	2	5	0	–
1955	25	Giants	38	34	2	14	16	.467	3.33	14	2	1	235.1	986	206	87	105	24	82	5	143	3	11	0	–
1956	26	Giants	41	36	5	20	13	.606	2.86	15	5	1	258.1	1,061	225	82	93	20	75	10	145	6	3	0	–
1957	27	Giants	40	30	6	12	18	.400	3.77	8	3	0	212.1	915	228	89	98	19	67	7	114	3	3	0	–
1958	28	Giants	41	34	5	16	13	.552	3.28	13	0	3	241.2	1,014	216	88	101	31	87	7	143	4	3	0	–
1959	29	Giants	40	38	1	19	10	.655	3.10	17	4	1	282.0	1,150	247	97	107	29	76	6	165	1	3	0	–
1960	30	Giants	41	10	19	6	7	.462	3.77	1	1	11	112.1	480	106	47	51	7	47	10	57	1	2	0	–
1961	31	Indians	11	7	0	0	4	.000	6.56	0	0	0	48.0	225	68	35	39	8	18	0	23	1	1	0	–
1961	31	Braves	9	0	4	1	0	1.000	7.59	0	0	0	10.2	51	16	9	9	2	3	0	8	0	0	0	–
12 Years			377	268	61	126	110	.534	3.34	102	25	21	1,992.1	8,424	1,870	739	860	186	687	45	1,162	27	38	1	–

LEGEND

G = Games; GS = Games Started; GF = Games Finished; W = Wins; L = Losses; PCT = Percentage;

ERA = Earned Run Average; CG = Complete Games; SHO = Shutouts; SV = Saves; IP = Innings Pitched;

BF = Batter Faced; H = Hits; ER = Earned Runs; R = Runs; HR = Home Runs; BB = Bases on Balls;

IBB = Intentional Bases on Balls; SO = Strikeouts; WP = Wild Pitches; HBP = Hit By Pitch; BK = Balks; HLD = Holds

HITTING STATS

Year	Age	Team	G	AB	R	H	2B	3B	HR	RBI	BB	SO	SH	SF	HBP	GIDP	AVG	OBP	SLG
1948	18	Braves	4	0	0	0	0	0	0	0	0	0	0	-	0	0	.000	.000	.000
1949	19	Braves	22	25	0	3	0	0	0	0	1	9	5	-	0	0	.120	.154	.120
1950	20	Braves	20	16	1	2	0	0	0	1	0	3	0	-	0	1	.125	.125	.125
1953	23	Braves	31	62	7	11	2	0	0	4	3	14	4	-	0	0	.177	.215	.210
1954	24	Giants	39	98	6	16	0	0	2	9	4	25	4	0	0	2	.163	.196	.224
1955	25	Giants	38	82	8	17	1	0	4	15	3	18	3	2	0	1	.207	.230	.366
1956	26	Giants	49	89	7	14	3	0	3	4	2	26	6	0	0	2	.157	.176	.292
1957	27	Giants	47	72	8	11	0	1	3	8	8	19	1	1	0	1	.153	.235	.306
1958	28	Giants	47	84	9	19	2	1	1	7	2	26	5	0	0	4	.226	.244	.310
1959	29	Giants	43	101	4	16	2	0	2	10	1	26	5	0	1	2	.158	.175	.238
1960	30	Giants	42	34	2	8	0	1	0	1	2	6	1	0	0	2	.235	.278	.294
1961	31	Indians	12	15	4	4	2	0	0	0	0	3	1	0	0	0	.267	.267	.400
1961	31	Braves	9	1	0	0	0	0	0	0	0	0	0	0	0	0	.000	.000	.000
12 Years			403	679	56	121	12	3	15	59	26	175	35	3	1	15	.178	.209	.271

LEGEND

G = Games; AB = At Bats; R = Runs; H = Hits; 2B = Doubles; 3B = Triples; HR = Home Runs; RBI = Runs Batted In;

BB = Base on Balls; SO = Strike Outs; SH = Sacrifice bunts ; SF = Sacrifice flies; HBP = Hit By Pitch;

GIDP = Ground Into Double Play; AVG = Average; OBP = On Base Percentage; SLG = Slugging Percentage

HONORS AND MISCELLANEOUS ITEMS

- One of only 17 players in Major League history to have never spent a single day in the minor leagues.
- One of only two pitchers in Major League history to record a win and a save in both the World Series and All-Star Game competition (Hall of Fame relief pitcher Bruce Sutter is the other).
- Sporting News Major League Pitcher of the Year (1954).
- Led National League in winning percentage (.750) and earned run average (2.30) in 1954.
- Led National League in shutouts in 1954 (6) and 1959 (4).
- Finished third in National League Most Valuable Player Award voting (1954).
- Finished third in the voting for the Hickok Belt Award as top professional athlete of the year (1954).
- Had a complete-game victory and a save while recording a 0.84 earned run average in the Giants' 1954 World Series sweep of Cleveland.
- Named to the National League All-Star team six times – 1954, 1956, 1957, 1958, and twice in 1959, when two All-Star games were staged. Was awarded a save in the 1956 game and a victory in the first game played in 1959.
- Won 20 or more games twice (1954 & 1956).
- Teamed with fellow 19-year-old Del Crandall during the 1949 season to become the youngest batterymates (pitcher and catcher) to combine for a Major League victory.
- Pitched the final game ever played by the New York Giants at the Polo Grounds (1957).
- Played for two franchises that moved from their original cities – the Braves from Boston to Milwaukee and the Giants from New York to San Francisco.
- Part of inaugural induction class of the Frontier Field Walk of Fame (Rochester sports Hall of Fame) in 1997.
- Part of inaugural induction class of the Section V (Western New York State) Baseball Hall of Fame in 2010.
- 2004 recipient of the Casey Stengel "You Could Look It Up" Award presented by the New York chapter of the Baseball Writers of America.

TRADES

FEBRUARY 1, 1954: Antonelli was dealt by the Milwaukee Braves with Billy Klaus, Don Liddle, Ebba St. Claire and $50,000 to the New York Giants in exchange for Bobby Thomson and Sam Calderone.

DECEMBER 3, 1960: Traded by the San Francisco Giants with Willie Kirkland to the Cleveland Indians for Harvey Kuenn.

JULY 4, 1961: Purchased by the Milwaukee Braves from the Cleveland Indians.

OCTOBER 11, 1961: Purchased by the New York Mets from the Milwaukee Braves.

ACKNOWLEDGMENTS

The authors would like to thank the following people for their assistance in helping this book become a reality:

Molly Cort, Marnie Soom, David Pankow and Laura DiPonzio Heise from RIT Press for their belief in this project and their professionalism and graciousness;

Sarah Freligh for her meticulous, eagle-eyed copy editing;

Gail Harms Antonelli for procuring photographs, arranging interviews and proofing the original manuscript;

Tim Wiles, Bill Francis and Pat Kelly from the Baseball Hall of Fame & Museum for answering research questions and finding photographs;

Steve Bradley, Bob Matthews, Dennis Floss from the Rochester *Democrat and Chronicle* for tracking down photographs.

ABOUT THE AUTHORS

Johnny Antonelli, a Rochester, New York, native, was one of baseball's top pitchers in the 1950s, twice winning more than twenty games and twice leading the National League in shutouts. His best season occurred in 1954 when he won twenty-one games and recorded a victory and a save in the World Series for the New York Giants. Following a career that saw him earn five All-Star nominations and record 126 victories, including twenty-five shutouts, Antonelli became a successful entrepreneur in the tire business. He and his wife Gail reside in Rochester and Santa Fe, New Mexico

Scott Pitoniak, a native of Rome, New York, and a magna cum laude graduate of Syracuse University, has written fifteen books. He has received more than a hundred writing awards during his sportswriting career. The Associated Press named him one of the top ten sports columnists in America and he is a member of three halls of fame. He and his wife, Beth, and children, Amy and Christopher, reside in Rochester.

INDEX